P9-CCO-760

THE CAT WHO'LL LIVE FOREVER

Also by Peter Gethers

The Dandy
Getting Blue
The Cat Who Went to Paris
A Cat Abroad

Written as Russell Andrews

Gideon
Icarus

The Final Adventures

of

NORTON

the Perfect Cat,

and

His Imperfect Human

Peter Gethers

THE CAT WHO'LL LIVE

FOREVER

Broadway Books
· New York ·

BROADWAY

THE CAT WHO'LL LIVE FOREVER. Copyright © 2001 by Peter Gethers.
All rights reserved. Printed in the United States of America. No part
of this book may be reproduced or transmitted in any form or by
any means, electronic or mechanical, including photocopying,
recording, or by any information storage and retrieval system,
without written permission from the publisher. For information,
address Broadway Books, a division of Random House, Inc.,
1540 Broadway, New York, NY 10036.

Broadway Books titles may be purchased for business or promotional use
or for special sales. For information, please write to: Special Markets
Department, Random House, Inc., 1540 Broadway,
New York, NY 10036.

BROADWAY BOOKS and its logo, a letter B bisected on the diagonal, are
trademarks of Broadway Books, a division of Random House, Inc.

"Recalling a Cat Who Got Around" by J. Barron, from the *New York
Times,* 5/12/1999. Reprinted with permission of the *New York Times.*

Visit our website at www.broadwaybooks.com

Library of Congress Cataloging-in-Publication Data

Gethers, Peter.
The cat who'll live forever: the final adventures of Norton, the
perfect cat, and his imperfect human / Peter Gethers.—1st ed.
p. cm.
1. Gethers, Peter. 2. Novelists, American—20th century—Biography.
3. Cat owners—United States—Biography. 4. Cats—United States—
Anecdotes. 5. Automobile travel—United States. 6. Scottish Fold cat.
I. Title.
PS3557.E84 Z47 2001
818'.5403—dc21
[B]
2001025450

FIRST EDITION

Designed by Judith Stagnitto Abbate/Abbate Design

ISBN 0-7679-0637-3

1 3 5 7 9 10 8 6 4 2

CONTENTS

DEDICATION

There's only one possible choice for this . . .

To the greatest little cat there ever was.
Au revoir, pal o' mine.

ACKNOWLEDGMENTS

've got to thank everyone who helped and loved my amazing Scottish Fold. Particularly Dr. Jonathan Turetsky, Dr. Andrew Pepper, Dr. Dianne DeLorenzo, and Dr. Marty Goldstein. I'd also like to thank all those who greeted him on his travels and took care of him along the way—but to list them all would take pages and pages and would need a better memory than mine.

For this book in particular, I'd like to thank Steve Rubin, the perfect publisher, Lauren Marino, the perfect editor, Esther Newberg, the perfect agent (and the only person who blubbered more than I did during this whole process), and Leona Nevler, because no one would be reading about Norton if it weren't for her.

Thanks, too, to all those who let me write about them, particularly my dear old mom and my dear young girlfriend.

FOREWORD

One of the reasons I moved to where I live now is because it's right near Washington Square Park, in the heart of Greenwich Village, and ever since I came to New York City, this is exactly where I fantasized about living. For human beings, however, wanting to do something and actually doing it are often two very different things. Which leads me to confess that the *real* reason I finally made the move is because my cat wanted to live on Washington Square Park.

Do me a favor and please don't ask how I know that this was his abode of choice. I know many strange things about my cat and I'd rather not discuss them because anyone who's not a cat fanatic will think I'm insane and anyone who is a cat fanatic (or has read about my particular fanaticism) will not even question the above statement. In fact, the only question those readers might ask is, "What took you so long?"

What took me so long was that I never realized that Norton, my exceptional, geniuslike—and did I mention dashingly handsome?—Scottish Fold pal, liked the dog run quite as much as he did.

My ignorance lasted until one day, when we were strolling around the Village on a sunny afternoon. Well, *I* was strolling; Norton was in his usual position, relaxing, half in, half hanging out of his cloth-and-mesh bag that hung on my shoulder, swivelling his head at everyone and everything around him. At some point we found ourselves in the middle of the park. In addition to the sounds of guitars and bongos (I know it sounds like you've suddenly been plunged into a Dobie Gillis episode, but I swear there really were guitars and bongos), there was also the distinct and incessant sound of dogs barking. We made our way to the south side of the square and, sure enough, there was this caged-in stretch of land—some grass, mostly dirt—in which twenty or thirty dogs of all shapes and sizes were rolling, running, jumping, fetching, yapping, growling, howling and generally acting like happy, idiotic canines. Norton was fascinated by this undignified but free-spirited behavior, so we mosyed up as close as we could to the wire fence that separated the dogs and their owners from non-dog-owning humans. Norton twisted himself further out of his bag, sticking his head—which would easily have fit whole into most of those dogs' mouths—as far across the boundary as he could muster. Several of the dogs raced over and barked hysterically but Norton stayed fairly serene, safe in the knowledge that none of the barkers could quite reach

him and, if they could, all I had to do was take a step backward and he'd be out of harm's way.

I knew he was enjoying all this so I found a nearby
bench, sat, and spent a decent part of the afternoon watching him watch the dogs. (I think I'll skip over the fact of
how much time I've actually spent during my adult years
doing nothing but watch my cat do things that most people would not find all that entertaining. All I'll say, so I keep
some modicum of self-respect, is that I'm a total Knicks fanatic and I tend to live and die with that very aggravating
basketball team. Nonetheless, if forced to choose, I'd have
to say, "Watching Norton do just about anything, one;
watching Latrell Sprewell juke to the basket, two.") A few
days later we went back to the same bench and my little pal
seemed to have just as good a time, so after that we started
going more often. And very soon after that I bought my
new apartment, which I tell people I bought because it's
right on Washington Square Park but which I really bought
because it's only about fifty yards from the dog run. Even
though I don't have a dog.

Once we were so conveniently located, Norton and I
went by there almost daily. We liked to take little strolls together in the afternoon; it got me away from the stress of sitting at my computer for hours on end and it got him away
from the stress of . . . well . . . napping by my computer for
hours on end. After a few weeks, we didn't just sit on the
bench on the outsider side of the fence, we started sitting inside the dog run. At first, the regular inhabitants (both human and canine) were not thrilled to see a feline intruder.
They (the canines, not the humans) would come running
up, barking ferociously, and my cat would retreat hastily into

his bag. But gradually, the ferocity stopped and curiosity took over, and then it was even possible to spot a kind of friendly wariness. Norton, throughout this process, usually just nestled calmly on my lap, half in, half out of his bag.

One day, the two of us were sitting in the sun, in the middle of the dog run, and a woman came in and sat down beside us. I was reading, Norton was sitting on my lap, totally out of his bag now, soaking in the rays. The dogs were basically ignoring us, except for one small one, a Scottie, I think, who didn't seem to understand that Norton wasn't a dog, because he couldn't seem to comprehend why Norton had zero interest in running around and playing fetch with him. The woman next to us sat there quite a long time; I was vaguely aware that she kept staring over in my direction. Then, finally, she nudged me. When I looked up, she didn't make a big deal out of it, she just said, "That's Norton, isn't it?" I nodded once, muttered something like, "Yup," then she didn't say anything else for a while. She did start nodding, though, repeatedly, as if finally grasping some long-sought knowledge. Then, her head still bobbing slowly, her voice betraying just the tiniest bit of awe, she said, "So it's true . . ."

I knew immediately what she meant. She had read about Norton. She had heard about him. His travels, his adventures, his remarkable effect on everyone around him. And now she had seen him in the flesh (or the fur, as it were), which is all it ever really took for people to understand how genuinely special he was.

I looked at my little cat and patted him on the head. My hand lay there, taking comfort in the smallness and the familiar fit within my palm.

"Yes," I said, smiling down at my beloved gray pal, "it's definitely true."

CHAPTER 1

A
CAT RETHOUGHT

E ver since I made the decision to write
this, the third book about my gray, floppy-eared
Scottish Fold pal, Norton, I have been trying to decide exactly how to begin.

That very human, very non-cat-like flaw called overthinking settled in all too quickly, and, as a result, more and
more time passed while I sat, stared into space, and didn't
type. This book would, I thought, for many reasons, be
somewhat different from the others and there were distinct
choices that had to be made. Each choice would clearly alter
style, tone and philosophy, if I can be pretentious enough to
suggest that the books about my cat actually *have* a philosophy (and, please, don't worry; believe me, I know enough to
understand that I'm writing something much closer to
Tuesdays with Norton than I am to *Meowing and Nothingness*).

My first instinct was to begin like this:

One of the reasons I became a writer is because using words the way I do is as close as I can get to putting some kind of order in this rather crazy world of ours.

I was then going to go on and describe that one of the things in life that drives me most crazy is the way the English language is constantly mangled. As always, this is an area in which we should learn from the feline way of doing things. Cats have a way of speaking that is direct and unmistakably clear. Their words might all be the same but the meanings behind them are just a tad less ambiguous than human-speak. There is no mistaking a meow that means "feed me" for one that means "scratch my stomach." Has anyone who has been owned by a cat for any length of time ever confused an "it's nice sitting by the fire" meow for one that says "let me out" or "sorry, there's no way I'm going to the vet"? The answer's no. Of course, not only is cat body language less inhibited than ours, cats tend to speak in commands, which does make life easier, at least for them. The only question I can come up with that a cat might ask is, "Are you okay?" And, if you're not, the follow-up meow is usually another directive: "Here, shove over so I can snuggle up to you and make you feel better." Cats have definitely gotten the act of communication down to an exact science.

But when humans open their mouths, the screw-ups are endless. The constant misuse of "I" for "me," for example (hint: If you don't wish for me to publicly humiliate you, never say "Just between you and I" or "Come with Freddy and I" in my presence). And the addition of the word "very" when describing something "unique." That's the same as saying "very one-of-a-kind" which is linguistically impossible. Then there's the fact that no one seems to know what the word "irony" means. It does not mean funny or snide or coincidental or satirical or anything along those lines. If you don't believe me, here's the definition straight from the *Random House Dictionary of the English Language*: "The use of words to convey a meaning that is the opposite of its literal meaning." If it's raining outside and you say, "Beautiful day, isn't it," that's irony. And the reason this matters to me is that the title of this book is, to a large extent, meant to be ironic, and it's important to understand that going in. Nothing and no one lives forever. Not plants, not people, and most unfortunate of all, not cats. In some ways, "life" itself is the ultimate ironic word because to live means that, eventually, you'll die. And that realization, that experience and understanding, is partly what this book is about.

But only partly.

I'm mainly trying to convey the feeling and the strength that come from being in contact with a truly amazing life force.

All of which is a long-winded way of explaining why my first choice for an opening didn't make the final cut. That and the fact that irony is not a concept that cats even understand. And although this book is written for humans, since cats can't read (unfortunately for me; if they could there's a reasonable chance I'd be the richest person on earth!), I didn't think it was appropriate to begin with something that went so against their nature.

A second possibility was to go for pure drama. For a long time, this was my intended first sentence:

On the day I moved into my dream apartment, I found out that my cat had cancer.

I'm sure you can see the value of that. I mean, it's definitely a grabber. And, like everything else I've ever written about Norton, it's true. But ultimately, I rejected that, too. Too sad. Too self-pitying. Way too cloyingly sentimental. And definitely *not* what this book is about. Most certainly not what Norton is about. What you're about to read is, I hope, anything but sad. It is not about illness, it is about health. Rather than the trauma of being sick, it is about the satisfaction and the bonds that arise as we age and learn how to care for each other—and learn how to accept that caring from others.

Anyone who has read earlier tales of life with Norton can tell you that I will almost always go for the gag—on paper and in life—and also that I am not a big fan of fake sentiment (several ex-girlfriends would say I'm also not a fan of real sentiment). But I *am* a fan of genuine emotion and, luckily for me, rarely is that exclusive of laughter. So in no way is this book depressing. It is, I hope, hilarious and joyful and as life-affirming as it's possible to be without turning into a Steven Spielberg movie.

In a way, this rambling and overthinking has actually done what my two initial openings couldn't possibly do. I did manage to bring some order, not just to this book but to my thought process. And, probably more important, I realized that, despite what I wrote earlier, the title is not really ironic.

The more I thought about it, the more I understood that in many ways my little gray pal will indeed live forever. And live exactly the way he'd like to: bringing pleasure and, on occasion, even meaning into other people's lives. I guess that's why, when push came to shove, I decided that what this book really is about is quite simple.

It's about my cat, Norton.

Exactly the same as the other two books. And that's why the real opening is as follows:

The wonderful thing about having a relationship with a cat—one of the many wonderful things about having a relationship with a cat—is that you never have a clue where that relationship will lead you . . .

CHAPTER 2

A CAT REVISITED

The wonderful thing about having a relationship with a cat—one of the *many* wonderful things about having a relationship with a cat—is that you never have a clue where that relationship will lead you. It can, and often does, lead toward love. But it can also lead toward frustration. And sometimes heartache. Or comfort. It can lead toward other relationships, feline as well as human. Sometimes it can lead to all of the above—in various combinations and even at the same time.

That relationship can also bring you to something truly extraordinary and life-changing, as has been the case with my extraordinary and life-changing Scottish Fold, Norton.

If you've read the many words I've already written about my amazing pal over the years, you won't need to be convinced of his ability to astound. You have already witnessed how he is—in no small way—responsible for my love life, my house, my travels, my professional success, and whatever emotional maturity I've managed to achieve. If you haven't read my rapturous descriptions, here's a little something to chew on (or scratch on, as the case may be) . . .

The backstory:

When we first met book publisher and writer Peter, he was your basic, insensitive oaf. Also a cat hater.

Enter Norton, age six weeks, a gift from one of Peter's girlfriends, Cindy.

Cindy goes. Norton stays. Peter becomes so attached to his kitten it borders on insanity (but is also totally deserved). Many other girlfriends come. Many other girlfriends go. Norton clearly has to take things into his own paws if he's ever going to have a stable home life.

Peter has to travel for business. So Norton travels with him. This changes in the years to come. *Norton* eventually has to travel for business so Peter travels with *him*. They go to Fire Island (Norton is stunned by how low his owner will sink to get a date for New Year's Eve), California (Norton meets the folks), Vermont (Norton goes cross-country skiing), Florida (Norton goes to a spring-training baseball game and becomes a huge fan of Andres "El Grand Gato" Galarraga. He also falls through the roof of a hotel restaurant, scaring two old ladies to death). There's much time spent in Paris (Norton greets Harrison Ford with a . . . um . . . *petit morceau de la merde dans la baignoire*. He also scares away a luscious Danish model and goes clubbing with Roman Polanski), and a sojourn in Amsterdam

(Norton goes to the taping of a topless Dutch TV quiz show—see, now aren't you sorry you didn't read the first book?!). Peter takes up with Janis, with Norton starring in the crucial matchmaking role of Dolly Levi. Peter buys Norton a house in Sag Harbor. Peter deals with the death of his father. Peter, thanks to you-know-who, finally understands what love is.

And then Peter writes a book called *The Cat Who Went to Paris*, which is about all of the above, and Norton becomes the Tom Cruise of cats. Also the William Styron of cats, since most true fans of the book are convinced he dictated the whole thing to Peter, who merely used his opposable thumbs to get himself a book contract.

Thanks to Tom . . . uh, Norton . . . Peter gets to spend a year in Provence, observing and chronicling the further adventures of his gray, folded-eared friend. In France, a chef at a three-star restaurant creates a marzipan mouse for Norton's pleasure. The sweetest cat in the world almost starts World War III in Italy over an uneaten sardine. In addition, Norton also rides a camel (don't ask), goes to Spain, suns himself in Sicily, tours the cathedrals of the Loire valley, skis in the French Alps, visits Anne Frank's house in Amsterdam and, back in southern France, charms the most charming village in the Luberon Valley.

Then it's back home. Which means New York City and Sag Harbor, Long Island.

Peter writes *A Cat Abroad*. It wins the Nobel Prize, the Pulitzer Prize, and is on the *New York Times* bestseller list for over four years (I just wanted to see if you were paying attention. The first sentence in this paragraph is true. The rest is a slight exaggeration).

In the first book, Peter learned about love from

Norton. In the second book, Peter learned about life. Peter decides there will be no third book because he thinks he has nothing left to learn from his cat . . .

We're up to Norton's tenth birthday, which is a little over eight years ago.

Which is where I left off.

And which is where I'll begin now. And the reason there is a Book #3 is because several years ago, I learned there was indeed one more very important thing I had to learn from my beloved little cat.

Maybe the most important thing of all . . .

CHAPTER 3

AN
AMERICAN CAT

Both cat and human had to make a fairly big adjustment to life upon returning to America from a year in the south of France. Norton had to readjust to chowing down on regular cat food (no combo cans of *lapin et foie*, his very favorite). His dad had to get used to working like a real person again. I also had to realize that I could no longer mutter any snide thing I wanted to in public, since now people could actually understand English.

In other words, we both had to prepare ourselves for being *normal* again, which was not my favorite situation to be in. Luckily for me, Norton made it very difficult to be absolutely normal.

When I first realized that life was truly going to be different on a permanent basis was when we went on our publicity tour for *A Cat Abroad*. I had been pretty amazed at the love and affection that had been showered upon my cat when Norton and I traveled together to promote *The Cat Who Went to Paris*—but that was nothing like this.

One of the first stops was Knoxville, Tennessee. At a Davis-Kidd bookstore, I gave my usual semi-witty speech and reading while Norton calmly sat by my side, in his favorite Sphinx-like pose, looking for all the world like he was my translator. When I was done talking, people lined up, ostensibly to have me sign their books but I'm sorry to say they didn't really care about my signature (or anything else about me). Oh, they were mostly polite, but they were all there to pet and talk to Norton. One man was so jazzed by the experience, he offered me a ticket to the city's biggest yearly event, the University of Tennessee–University of Florida football game, which was taking place the next day. When I thanked him but said, kiddingly, that I couldn't possibly go without my pal because he was a huge Tennessee fan, the man looked at Norton and said, "Hell, I'll get him a ticket, too." I have to say, it was tempting but I finally decided it was better that I stick to the tour schedule than take Norton to drink beer and eat hot dogs and root for UT.

One extremely nice, middle-aged woman came shyly forward when the crowd began to thin. She glanced at me, stared lovingly at you-know-who and said, "I drove over four hundred miles to see him." Her tone was even more reverential than her words. It was a lot like she was viewing the front of one of those refrigerators in someone's RV where the grease has coagulated into a vision of the Virgin Mary. It was so touching to see the attachment she had for my cat, I let her spend a few minutes alone with the star of the evening, who was extremely nice, purring contentedly during their chat. I don't know what they chatted about—and I don't think I want to know—but I can say with certainty that she was not at all disappointed. Afterward she thanked him, was thoughtful enough to thank me, too, then presumably drove another four hundred miles back home.

I happened to have good friends living in Knoxville then, Lee and Linda Eisenberg. Linda is an attractive, sweet, lovely woman and *everyone* adores her. Lee is a tad more cynical. And neurotic. And weird. And . . . well, let's just say that not counting his immediate family, about *three* people adore Lee. Luckily, I'm one of them. They are both transplanted New Yorkers and thus pretty much think they've seen it all. But even they were startled by what they witnessed and heard that night. Lee, who had spent much time with Norton before feline fame had set in, was a little taken aback by the fervor of his fans. He'd socialized with Norton in New York and also in Florida (on our annual spring training baseball trips) and I have a hunch he felt a little bit like he'd been dating Norma Jean Baker before she became Marilyn Monroe—it had been fine but who knew it was *so* fine? After the event, we went back to their Xanadu-like house where Linda made dinner. I think she was a bit surprised that, after all the adulation Norton had soaked up from his adoring public, he decided to revert to being a normal cat and, instead of joining us at the table, ate off a bowl on the floor. I have to admit, I was a little surprised myself.

The evening ended, after the delicious dinner, when Lee took me and Norton back to our hotel. We were dropped off—Lee still shaking his head and looking at

Norton as if he'd never seen him before—and headed up to
the room. As we passed the check-in desk, the woman
clerk behind the counter hesitated and then called out,
"Mr. Norton?" I immediately assumed that this was yet another nightmare to confront in my attempt to keep any of
my own ego intact—someone actually calling me by my
cat's name—but the fact is, she wasn't talking to me. She
was directly addressing the one of us with folded ears,
which I realized when I went over to her, started to say,
"Well, actually, my name's Gethers," and saw that she wasn't
even looking at me. She reached out to pet Norton in his
bag and said, looking into his eyes, "I'm a big fan. I just
wanted to let you know I'm sorry I couldn't go to your
reading. I had to work." I waited—as always, half-expect-
ing Norton to answer and say, "Oh, that's all right, my dear.
Care to join me in my shoulder bag for a bit of dry
food?"—but all he did was look up and give a solid purr as
her hand brushed across his soft fur. That seemed to be
enough for the woman desk clerk, however, who had an
expression on her face that I personally have never been
able to induce in any woman without saying the words
"tickets to the Caribbean."

While in Tennessee, we made a second stop—Memphis.
It was partly for the book tour and partly because a newspaper, the *New York Daily News*, had asked me to write an
article about traveling with Norton. Naturally, when the
editor called she asked if *Norton* could write an article for
the paper. When I determined that she wasn't joking, I explained to her about the whole opposable thumb thing and

finally she said, "Well, we'll let you do it but we really want *his* point of view." So in addition to letting his fans adore him, my assignment was to get Norton's reactions to the sights and sounds of Memphis.

Longtime and much loved girlfriend, Janis, grew up in Memphis, so she agreed to come down and meet me there. The three of us stayed at the Peabody Hotel, which is famous for its beauty, stateliness and ducks. Yes, you read that correctly. Every morning, at 9 A.M., the elevator doors open and a hotel employee leads a line of ducks out into the lobby where they waddle across the floor until they reach a large marble fountain. The ducks then step into the water, where they float around for the day in as dignified a manner as possible. At 6 P.M., they all hop out of their pool, reverse their path across the lobby and disappear back into the elevator. I don't know where they go from there, although I prefer to believe it's to their own suite rather than to some cage on the roof. What I do know is that Norton was absolutely fascinated by this daily ritual. We stayed there for two days and each morning he'd be on my shoulder, staring at the quackers as they paraded by. One afternoon, we were having a drink in the lobby—Norton loved the big comfortable seats—and he strolled over to the edge of the fountain and hopped up onto the little ledge. I suppose that a normal cat, staring at all those fowl, might have been thinking about an early supper. Norton did not have that lip-smacking look about him, however. He was mostly curious. I like to think that what he was pondering was how these ducks had somehow managed to get an even better gig than he'd gotten.

It was early summer when we were in Memphis, which meant that the temperature was only about three hundred degrees Fahrenheit. Janis had warned me about the heat down there and I had blown her off, explaining that I liked and thrived in all extreme temperatures. Which, for the most part, I do. Being in Memphis, though, was not a normal extreme. The only way I can describe walking out of the air-conditioned hotel lobby and into the Tennessee summer air is that it must be a lot like stepping directly into the bowels of hell. But step we did, because I wanted Norton to see Graceland, home of The King.

Elvis was a little before Norton's time—he was much more of an REM and Tom Petty fan—but I thought it would do him good to get a little rock and roll history. Unfortunately, we ran into a direct violation of the FRA—Feline Rights Amendment—and a blatant example of catism, when we were turned away at the door, told that cats were not allowed inside. It was a perfect example of how removed from reality we both were. Since he had dined in some of the best restaurants in the world and been welcomed in cathedrals and museums all over Europe, both Norton and I were astonished that he was barred from any public place, particularly one displaying more suede and velvet capes than any building east of the Liberace Museum. But, after a brief argument, we accepted our fate and turned bravely back into the blazing wall of heat that some people referred to as Memphis.

To make it up to my cat, whose feelings were clearly wounded, Janis's father, Marv, took us all to one of the great barbeque places in the world, Corky's (its only flaw is that, unlike some of the smaller, less commercial barbeque places in Memphis, they don't serve barbequed baloney). There, we escaped the shadow of Colonel Parker while Norton sat in his own chair, munched on some delicious pulled pork and took solace in the astonished murmurings of the waitress, who kept repeating, in her thick southern accent, "Ah nevah saw a cat eat bah-bee-cue befaw."

We more or less toured the country over the course of a couple of weeks. By this time, I had the routine down pat.

Publishers hire "escorts" to drive authors around in each city. These escorts not only make sure we arrive where we're supposed to—and arrive on time—they usually know all the key people at the newspaper offices and radio and TV stations, so they're familiar with the layouts and routines and generally are able to make everyone's life easier. Norton's life was made a lot easier by his escorts. We would leave Boston (or whatever city we were in) and fly to Dayton (or whatever city we were flying to). Driving *to* the airport, the escort would have a ready-to-use litter box in the back seat of the car, so Norton could . . . um . . . take advantage of it . . . up until the last possible moment before having to board the plane. When we arrived, we'd be picked up at the gate—I'd be easy to recognize; I was the one with a cat on his shoulder—then, driving *from* the airport, the new escort would also have a litter box all set up so Norton wouldn't have to miss a beat. I left several needed shirts back home, instead packing in my bag plenty of folding, portable litter boxes and a five- or ten-pound bag of litter, which I'd then set up in the hotel room the moment we arrived. No matter how good the traveler, traveling is hard on a cat, so I was determined to make my guy's life as cushy as possible during the ordeal. I was well aware of the favor he was doing for me, so I swore I'd put him to work only if he were exactly as comfortable as he'd be at home.

Norton's airplane rides were always a little easier than the norm because by this time word was out on the flight attendant circuit. He was often recognized and given VIP treatment. While other pets were usually stuffed under the seats in their carry-on bags, most of the time Norton was allowed to sit on my lap or on the seat next to me if it was empty. He was usually given some food and was always fussed over and petted. The only trade-off was that I had to hear many woeful—and long—tales from stewardesses about how much they missed their own cats. It was well worth it, however, and I know Norton appreciated my stoicism.

Since we lived in New York, it was simple to do publicity whenever we were there. One of Norton's easiest appearances was on a TV show called "The Pet Department" on the FX cable network. The taping went fine (Norton was a seasoned TV pro by this time; he seemed to know exactly when to listen and stay calm and exactly when to upstage me by being cute). The only notable oddity was in the itinerary that was given to me before the appearance. The publicist faxed over a piece of paper telling us where to go, when to arrive, how long the taping would take and who to ask for when I got there. And then at the bottom it said, "HOSTS: Steve Walker & Jack the dog."

Sure enough, when we showed up at the studio, some guy came up to me, said that his name was Steve and that he'd be doing the interview. And by his side, some fairly large dog walked up to Norton, sniffed around, then sat with us when the cameras were turned on and we chatted for the national audience. I must admit, I kept waiting for

Jack the dog to ask Norton about the pleasures of the Washington Square Park dog run, but both animals remained silent and let the humans talk.

I got a lot of similar publicity itineraries during this period. Almost all of them said, at the bottom: "Your escort is so-and-so. She will meet your flight and she will have a five-pound bag of cat litter in the car for you." Not exactly the stretch limo and Dom Perignon treatment, but it worked for me.

For Milwaukee, the publicist's instructions were typical of the way we were greeted. It was for a radio show hosted by Marilyn Mee. On the piece of paper it said: "Marilyn is a HUGE fan. She would like to take lots of pictures of Norton in the studio. She is the one who called to ask if she could conduct an interview with Norton Gethers."

It's the story of my postcat life, trust me.

At the book-signing event in Milwaukee, they had a Norton look-alike contest. Luckily for everyone, the contest wasn't actually held live while we were there; cat owners had submitted photos and Norton and I were supposed to pick the winner. The lucky look-alike won a gift certificate to the bookstore and a can of Pounce.

At all the book signing events, there was always a question and answer session at the end of my spiel. In general, I could anticipate what questions would be asked. There was always someone who wanted to know more about the whole portable litter box situation. Someone usually asked for Norton's key statistics: how old he was, how much he weighed, etc. There was often one person who would reprimand me for letting Norton explore the rooftops of Paris on his own, insisting that I was putting his life in danger. And there was, count on it, one person who would stand up, tell a very long story about his or her own cat, then sit down without asking any question at all. And then . . .

Well . . . there were always a few oddities.

In Seattle, someone asked for Norton's specific measurements. I mean, we're talking sleeve size. I had to admit that was one of the few things I didn't know about my cat, but I guess she was able to eyeball him sufficiently in person because a few weeks later I received a hand-knitted coat in the mail. Size extra-extra-extra-small.

In Boca Raton, a woman asked if I knew Norton's birth date and exact time of birth. The fact is, I did (well, not exact, but close enough), but I wanted to know why she was asking before I responded. She finally admitted that she wanted to do Norton's astrological chart and send it to him as a present. As gently as possible, I broke it to her that Norton did not believe in astrology and that she should skip the chart. I wouldn't have minded seeing her try to read his tarot cards, but I decided not to bring it up.

In San Francisco, the SPCA established a yearly "Norton Award" which stood for service dedicated to improving the lives of animals. I'm still not a hundred percent clear if the award is supposed to be given to humans or to animals but we decided not to ask and just be humble and gracious when the SPCA handed its certificate of merit to the only Scottish Fold cat in attendance at the ceremony.

Norton was very big in Ohio for some reason, so we went to various cities there—Dayton, Columbus and Cincinnati. One group of bookstore workers took him to an excellent pub in downtown Cincinnati to celebrate the occasion. In Columbus, where there are an incredible number of good bookstores, the escort took us around from store to store so clerks and salespeople could meet the famous cat. We were headed to the escort's car in the parking lot of one of the mall stores when two elderly women saw Norton perched in his shoulder bag. One woman came running—well, running may not be the right term, let's say inching—up to him. She began stroking his head and asked me if he was a Scottish Fold. When I said that he was, she got extremely excited and started saying to her friend, "Remember that book I was telling you about? Well this is the same kind of cat as the one who went to Paris." Then she turned to me and said, "He's exactly like the cat who went to Paris." I got the same thrilling rush as if someone had come up to me and asked how to get to Carnegie Hall. I got to smile and say to her, "Well, actually, he's not *like* the cat who went to Paris. He *is* the cat who went to Paris." She screeched and then took her hand away from his head, as if now too awed to touch him.

In Norfolk, Virginia, a bookseller had a good gimmick to help sales and keep her best customers loyal. Whoever bought the most books over a period of six months would get some kind of special reward or gift. Her gift this particular six-month period was a dinner with Norton. So when she picked us up at the airport, we checked in to our hotel, set up this night's litter box, then were whisked right out and taken to the best restaurant in town. There we dined with four of her best customers. The only catch was that each customer wanted to spend some individual time with Norton. Which meant that every twenty minutes or so, we had to move around the table so everyone had a chance to sit next to him. I happened to have an aunt, SaraLee, who was living in Norfolk with her new husband, Micky. I had asked if they could be invited to dinner and the bookstore owner was gracious enough to include them.

SaraLee had never met my cat and she was a little incredulous at the excitement he was stirring up at the dinner table. At the beginning, she announced that there was no need for her to move around to dine next to Norton, since she was really there to visit with her beloved nephew. However, after an hour of seeing the ecstatic expressions on everyone's face, when it came around to her, she looked at me apologetically and said, "I don't think I can pass this up." After dinner, when we said goodnight, she asked, "Does this happen to you all the time?" When I said that it did, she shook her head in wonder. But at least she finally understood what all the fuss was about.

Los Angeles was always a pleasure for Norton. The Four Seasons Hotel was like a home away from home for him. Whenever we drove up to the front, the parking guys would grab the luggage and say, "Nice to have you back, Norton." Walking inside was a little bit like what I always imagined would happen in the court of Louis XIV. No one exactly strewed flowers in Norton's path, but everyone from the concierge to the bellmen to the desk clerks would greet him by name and give him a rousing welcome. He was even allowed to use the pool on the fourth floor of the hotel (well, let's say he used the pool area; swimming was not one of my cat's preferred sports). One of my top ten favorite images of Norton is picturing him sitting out by that pool, relaxing on his own chaise lounge while a waiter would bring him over a small bowl of ice water.

Dining out in America was always a little tricky. It's against the health laws for non-seeing-eye animals to be inside a restaurant, so usually the restaurant owner has to give special permission (as happened in Norfolk) and be willing to risk the wrath of any government inspectors who might happen to wander in. In L.A., Norton was always welcome at the city's most popular restaurant, Spago. The owner, Wolfgang Puck, was a friend (and my mother writes his cookbooks; there's no question that she would like me better than she already does if I spoke with a hint of an Austrian accent and could cook squab the way Wolf does. Now that I think about it, Janis would also like me a lot better if I could cook *anything* the way Wolf does). Plus, Wolf's wife, Barbara, is the biggest animal nut around. She has a llama in her backyard, to illustrate my point, as well as the usual assortment of dogs and cats and God knows what else. When *The Cat Who Went to Paris* was published, we had the launch party at Spago and Wolf made Norton his own special pizza, covered with cat treats. I think they could get away with letting Norton eat in public because Spago is so hot—and tables there are in such demand—that Wolf probably has more clout than the mayor or governor. I mean, I'd hate to be a public official trying to get a table for four at 8 P.M. on a Saturday if that official was the person responsible for Norton's banishment.

This particular trip, there was a special request for dinner. In town at the same time was a very close friend, William Goldman, who is not only a writing idol of mine, he is a serious foodie. He wanted to take two women friends of his, Suzanne Goodson and Helen Bransford, to Spago and I agreed to make the reservation. Helen, who's also an animal nut—in case you think *I'm* weird, *she* often travels with her pet pig!—had heard that Norton was in town, so she got Bill to call me and ask if Norton could join them for their evening meal. As usual, I explained that if the cat came I had to come, too. Bill hesitated but said he supposed that would be fine (he didn't even check with Helen—he just took that heavy responsibility right on his own shoulders).

When we all sat down for dinner—Norton in his own chair, of course—the first thing that happened was that our waiter came over and said, "I don't know if you remember me, but I waited on you for Norton's book party. I had just started and that was my first celebrity event." He then looked down at Norton and said, "It's a pleasure to have you back."

During dinner, we all ordered various delicacies off the menu and, without even asking, the waiter brought over a plate of grilled chicken for Norton. Everything was absolutely delicious, but it was soon clear that Suzanne was not a happy camper. She kept looking over at Norton—I thought that perhaps she was allergic or disturbed by eating in such proximity to a four-legged furry guy. But no. What disturbed Suzanne, which she later confessed to Bill, was that Norton's food looked better than hers. All she had wanted to eat was grilled chicken—but it wasn't on the menu. And clearly Norton was the only one of us with enough clout to get a specially prepared meal.

After L.A., my little buddy and I drove down to San Diego. He was much beloved at Warwick's bookstore and we had a reading there. The appearance went as usual—

people tolerated and chuckled at my shtick then mobbed Norton in adulation. Afterward, we went to dinner at a friend's house, a literary agent named Margaret McBride. Margaret is quite successful and extremely popular, and she and her husband are the perfect hosts. That night, to celebrate Norton's appearance she had a particularly eclectic group of notable San Diegoans (San Diegites? San Diegpeople?). One of them was Audrey Geisel, a.k.a. Mrs. Dr. Seuss. Audrey was very taken with Norton and was rather shocked at how well behaved he was, which isn't so surprising, I guess, since her husband's most famous work was all about an anarchic cat who does his best to physically destroy house and home. I did feel some kind of psychic link, I must admit, between my fairly famous real cat and the wife of the creator of the world's most famous fictional feline. Showing my amazing maturity, I totally refrained from speaking in rhyme during the party or, when hors d'oeuvres were passed, from saying things like, "Gee, do you by any chance have any green eggs and ham?" I'm sure that Margaret was grateful for my restraint. I *know* that Norton was. There would be nothing worse for a cat than being embarrassed in front of the Seuss family.

The other guest of distinction that night was Alexander Butterfield. When I heard the name, it rang a bell but I couldn't quite place it. Then, as he began recounting a few anecdotes—mentioning several famous names, discussing a few historical events—it suddenly came to me. My amazing maturity and restraint immediately deserted me and I blurted out, "You're the guy who blew the whistle on Nixon!"

He was indeed the man who, when called before the

Watergate committee, had revealed one of the great secrets in history up to that point—that Richard Nixon, while president, taped every conversation he had in the oval office. It was, of course, those tapes that led to Nixon's downfall and if the man who was now busily fussing over my cat hadn't brought this to the public's attention, who knows how history would have been altered. Although Butterfield was a Nixon supporter and a devoted Republican, after the revelation he was not viewed kindly by those in the Nixon camp or by his fellow party members. He was vilified or revered, depending on your point of view, which is not always the most pleasant situation to be in. But to me the strangest thing is that he was famous only because he'd done something that everyone is supposed to do on a daily, regular basis—he told the truth, impartially and with no agenda. Just because it was the right thing to do. During dinner, he was extremely pleasant and entertaining. There was something inherently if quietly honorable about him, although at the same time also a touch sad. When we got back to our hotel room, I thought about explaining to Norton the vagaries of fame—the pitfalls and the dangers, the highs and lows—but by then he was already deeply asleep on the most comfortable chair in the room. I realized that, as with most other things, cats do not have to worry about human-style ups and downs. Cats are guileless. They do not need to tape their private conversations and they do not ostracize others of their species for speaking the truth. Cats are, by nature, truthful animals. In fact, cats do not know *how* to lie, which I'm sure is one of the reasons they are able to walk into hotel rooms and immediately fall asleep on the most comfortable chair.

That night, which was near the end of our tour, I decided I would not be audacious enough to explain to Norton about the fickle finger of fame. Instead I concluded that maybe I'd just pay closer attention, see how he coped with life, and do my best to learn from the master.

CHAPTER 4

A CAT
IN THE SPRING

When the book tour was over, I decided that it was time for one of us to retire. Since I could earn money without Norton but Norton was fairly dependent on me for his daily cans of food, the decision was an easy one. It only made sense that I be the one to remain, if you'll excuse a cat's most hated expression, in the rat race. This was not just a financial decision, though. Norton was getting on in years—he was ten at this point—and I very much wanted him to spend the rest of his life in comfort and ease. So, *voilà*, just like that, his life as a literary lion (okay, not exactly a lion, but you'll have to excuse the feline exaggeration; it sounded too good to pass up) was over.

That didn't mean it was the end of his traveling days, however. Those were, by no means, over.

What I'm about to launch into right now might sound like a digression, but trust me, it's a relevant if circuitous way to get back to Norton's traveling. It's also as good an explanation as I can come up with as to why I value the time spent with him so very much.

I'm not in any way, shape or form a religious person. Some readers have already figured this out for themselves because over the years, while I've received thousands of enthusiastic and warm-hearted letters from people who have grown to love Norton, I've also received a much smaller if more vociferous share of really negative, sometimes downright nasty letters. And I'm sorry to say that every one of the latter has been the result of my fairly benign comments about religion.

I've gotten several notes telling me that because of my flippancy and irreverency, Norton was surely going to heaven and I was just as surely going in the far opposite direction (most of these letters actually use phrases like "the far opposite direction"; they're too frightened to even write the word "hell"). Several people skipped over the promise of heaven for my cat and wrote just for the pleasure of letting me know that I was damned and doomed. I've received quite a few pages of scripture from people hoping to educate me or change my thinking (and for anyone who's considering sending more, I should probably let you know that I don't read these pages; as long as I'm going to be roasting on a spit for eternity anyway, I figure it won't really hurt me any further to crumple them up and toss them away. Sometimes, just to tempt fate, I also think impure thoughts while I'm doing that). I've gotten several letters telling me that the writers enjoyed my books immensely until they got to a joke or what they perceived as a snide comment about God, at which point those same books wound up in the trash (For the public record, they were right, those comments *were* snide. If any of those people who were offended went out and bought this book anyway, I guess this is as good a time to break it to you that I meant what I said then and I mean it now. So go back to the bookstore and get your money back before you read any further and work yourself up into another hysterical frenzy). I got one letter from a couple who read *A Cat Abroad* aloud to each other in the car every day while they commuted from home to work. That reading stopped, however, when they reached some paganlike observation and almost drove the car off the side of the road. Quite recently I received a note from a woman who blamed me for corrupting America's youth. Her accusation came about because she was horrified to read that Janis and I slept in the same bed without being married. I certainly don't want to give Janis a swelled head, but I've got to say, again for the record, that horrified woman doesn't know what she's missing! And I have additional bad news for this woman: Norton and I *also* spent many years in the same bed without being married. Not only that, he licked me quite a bit. Sometimes right on the lips!

For anyone who's still with me, what I object to most about religion is not the actual faith or belief in a supreme being or guiding force. That's just fine with me. It's the bigotry and hypocrisy that too often ensue from such blind faith. As always, let us learn from cats, those most unhypocritical of creatures, who, as far as we know, do not attend church or temple or any other restrictive place of worship that doesn't have a food dish readily available. To take the analogy one step further, it's also fairly difficult to imagine a cat agreeing to slay, persecute, maim, torture, hate or ridicule millions of its own species throughout history because they refuse to acknowledge the presence of some sort of invisible, all-knowing tiger who supposedly lives up in the sky.

Cats never let symbols assume importance over reality, which is what happens when religion or just about anything else becomes institutionalized. And I'm fairly certain that any self-respecting feline would agree with my dislike of anything that relieves us from responsibility for our own actions or that exists only to help us escape into an unreal sense of safety. I also do not believe, as many of my two-legged, nonfurry friends do when explaining their attendance of religious ceremonies, in using the excuse that religion provides a sense of community. Thanks, but no thanks. I much prefer choosing my own community, based on real ties and legitimate connections.

What I *do* understand—don't worry, I'm not a total iconoclastic moron—is the concept of rituals. I've got plenty of them that I adhere to and love. But—and this is a big but; feel free to call me a kook—I prefer to create my own rituals and to do them with friends rather than strangers who happen to have some distant relatives who once worshiped the same human, goat or big, hairy guy with a scythe who drinks nectar all day up on Mount Olympus. Rather than fasting on a randomly chosen day or confessing once a week to expunge my sins, I prefer to ritualize things that I enjoy, that have a personal meaning and provide genuine pleasure—spiritual, intellectual or physical. That includes things like having Thanksgiving dinner with the same group of close friends every year, and an annual New Year's Day hike in Provence with a different but equally close group of friends, and a regular Final Four trip to Las Vegas with a bunch of guys who like to gamble and talk like the Rat Pack for forty-eight hours straight.

Do you see where this is leading?

No, probably not.

Well, the point is that every April, Janis and I indulge in one of my favorite rituals, which is to go on a spring trip with a group of ten or twelve close friends. We pick a spot, usually in America, where few of us have been, and we go there for a long weekend to do some sightseeing, some fine dining and drinking, and enjoy each other's company. Now *that's* my idea of a meaningful ritual.

Especially when accompanied by my very favorite traveling companion.

The first Spring Trip was down to New Orleans. We did not know the whole group excursion was going to become a ritual then; it was meant to be a one-shot. Janis and I arranged almost everything that year because the idea was to celebrate my birthday (since then, a different person is responsible for the grunt work for each trip). We rented out the LaMothe House, a small shabbily elegant hotel in the French Quarter. And, a week or so before we left, I established another yearly ritual by having a lengthy phone conversation with the hotel manager, trying to convince her to allow a cat to stay there as one of their guests. In the years to come, the hotel employee on the other end of the phone would occasionally say, "Oh sure, we love cats. No problem." More often, it was an, "Absolutely not. We do not allow pets and it's out of the question." I would then assure the place that I would pay for any possible damages or cleaning bills (although there never were any of either; Norton was both tidy and considerate of other people's property). I would also offer to pay extra for the additional guest (even though Norton didn't require his own room, bed, towels or food; at most, he needed two small bowls, one for water, one for nourishment, that could be kept in the bathroom). If none of that worked, I'd pull out the big gun: I'd mention Norton's name. Ninety-nine percent of the time that would do the trick and I'd hear the voice on the other end of the phone say, "Oh, Norton—well, Norton's *different*."

In New Orleans, that first trip, the hotel grudgingly allowed my cat to come, although they made it very clear they didn't approve. But after only one weekend in his presence, they changed their tune—big time. It changed so much that a couple of years later, when Janis and I were planning to go back to New Orleans and called to make a reservation at the same hotel, the manager begged me to bring Norton along. "We're still talking about him," she said. "And we'd be *very* pleased if he'd grace us with his presence."

Everyone who went with us to New Orleans felt that way about Norton. The weekend was extraordinarily fun, made more so by the fact that almost everywhere we went, so did my purring pal. Because we all had such a good time eating like pigs (particularly at Emeril's, where I thought Norton might pass out from the ecstasy of eating the salmon cheesecake), going to antebellum plantations, sipping chicory-flavored coffee and visiting the Voodoo Museum, we decided to repeat the experience the following spring and try traveling to Charleston, South Carolina.

Before departing, I had another long discussion with someone at the small hotel we wanted to stay at. This person was even more adamant that Norton should not come a callin'. Eventually, I wore him down but when we showed up the people at the hotel were so wary and disapproving that they made sure, when we checked in, to include a stern lecture about making Norton stay in his room at all times. Well, all I can say is that we all loved the city of Charleston—we went on garden and house tours, ate well, just enjoyed walking around one of the truly charming cities in the world—but by far the best part was watching what happened at the hotel. At our first breakfast there, Norton snuck downstairs and tried to join us for the morning meal. The manager came in to shoo him out, saw him sitting calmly in his chair and wound up petting him and deciding he was a perfectly fine breakfast guest. Before we went out to dinner that night, all the travelers—including the one feline—met for a drink in the lobby. When it was time to leave for the restaurant, I went to take Norton back up to our room (he was bushed and the restaurant wasn't thrilled about experiencing the pleasures of indoor cat dining). Before I got to the first step, the man at the front desk stopped me and, hemming and hawing, finally said that if I wanted to leave my cat downstairs, he'd be more than happy to keep him company for a little while. That little while turned into the entire evening. When we came back from dinner, there was Norton sitting on the front desk, being petted by the clerk, as well as a few other hotel workers and guests. The clerk explained that Norton was such good company it had seemed a shame to lock him in upstairs, so the staff agreed that they should just let him stick around until we returned. The third and final day we were there, Norton didn't come touring with us at all. He spent the day at the front desk, welcoming new guests and keeping the hotel staff company. I suspect that more than a few tears were shed when we packed our bags and headed back up north.

Over the next few years, the same group, with a few additions and subtractions—some people dropped out, some got married and fell out of the group, some just didn't have room for another ritual in their lives—ventured to San Francisco and the Napa wine country, the Brandywine country in Pennsylvania, the eastern shore of Maryland, Savannah, Georgia and Key West. Norton went almost everywhere with us and, in each place, not only made the trip much more enjoyable for us all, he spread that pleasure to the people we met and came to know along the way.

One of the best weekends—for people and cat—was at a wonderful farmhouse bed-and-breakfast called Sweetwater Farm in the Brandywine country of Pennsylvania.

Janis and I decided to drive there, since the B&B was only an hour and a half or so from New York. There were five of us in the car: me, Janis, my mom and her older sister, Belle (both of whom came to New Orleans for my birthday and had become very popular regulars for these trips), and Norton.

Belle, who was then eighty years old, was an interesting and exceptional person, smart, funny, wickedly acerbic, extraordinary generous, very, very tough, and startlingly truthful. (We were once discussing an acquaintance of my mother's and, trying to be pleasant, I said that she was a nice person. Belle said, "Yeah, if you happen to like stupid, lazy and ugly." I stared at her, somewhat aghast, although her description was 100 percent accurate, and she followed it with, "I'm too old to beat around the bush.") She smoked a ton and had that deep, throaty, smoker's voice that sounded like she had a ton of gravel in her throat, and because she couldn't ever remember anyone's name she used to greet everyone with a raspy, "Hiya, darling." I think I'm making her sound a little bit like William Demarest with a wig on and, now that I think of it, that description's not too far off base. That first year in New Orleans, at our Saturday night dinner at Emeril's, a cloth napkin was passed around the table and everyone signed it with some kind of witty birthday greeting. Belle wrote: "Happy to be here. At my age, happy to be *anywhere*." That instantly became the slogan for that and all future trips. We even printed up buttons for the next year's excursion with Belle's picture and that phrase printed on them.

When the New Orleans weekend was over, my mother went back home to her house in Los Angeles. Belle lived in New York but went with her, a continuation of her vacation. I called my mom a day or two after their return to report that all of my friends—most of whom met Belle for the first time down south—were thrilled that they both had come. They were all particularly impressed that Belle had stayed up as late as we had, walked everywhere we walked, done everything we did and, most impressive of all, drunk everything we drank (Belle, who lived for her daily afternoon glass—or glasses, as the case may be—of scotch, could drink all of us under the table, and pretty much did all weekend. The big drink in New Orleans is something called a Hurricane, a lethal mixture of fruit juices and rum and God knows what else. At one bar, Belle decided that this was something she had to try, but she asked the bartender if he could make a "scotch Hurricane." The bartender had his doubts, it was clear, but did as he was told. Belle proclaimed the concoction delicious—and had two). My mother turned to her sister to repeat the accolades from the East Coast and, in the background, I could hear Belle, indignant rather than pleased at the compliments, say, "What's the big deal? What do they think I am—*ninety*?!"

Belle was the person closest to my mother in their family. Even though my mom was then nearly seventy, she was still the little sister and Belle was quite protective. Belle was the protector of the whole family, in fact, the glue that held them all together. Part of it was due to her background. She was a Depression child, the fourth of six children, and the one who consistently got the worst deal. There was an older brother, who got better treatment simply because he was a boy. There were two older sisters. One was absolutely stunning looking, so she got away with murder. One was smart, so a lot of good things came her way. Then came Belle who, thanks to the onrush of the Depression, was the only child who didn't get to go to college and was forced to work early and continuously. By the time my mother and her younger brother were around, after a gap of quite a few years, the country's hard times were ending and normal life was resumed, so the two "babies" of the family also escaped most of the hardships that Belle had to endure. As a result of timing and the era and certain choices Belle made throughout her life, by the time she was eighty she was tough, independent, deeply cynical and mostly fearless.

I say "mostly" because she was absolutely terrified of one thing and one thing only.

You got that right . . .

Cats.

Which meant that she was horrified when she realized that she didn't only have to drive to Sweetwater Farm with a litter box by her feet, she had to drive with a cat perched mere inches away. She had spent time with Norton before, but always at a distance. Never in such proximity.

We started with Belle and my mother in the back seat. I drove. Janis sat in the passenger seat with Norton on her lap. Normally, Norton would have been happy as could be sitting up front (He was usually not allowed; that was Janis's law—she thought it was too dangerous. I, of course, always wanted him as close as possible. Norton knew that, so when it was just the three of us, he'd wait until Janis fell asleep, then he'd instantly sneak into the front seat and sit on my lap or, his preferred choice of seating, my shoulder). This trip, however, Norton sensed hostility from somewhere in the car. It was a challenge he could never resist. So he kept trying to move to the back seat where he could settle onto the ledge by the back windshield and try to convert Belle from foe to friend. The first half hour or so was mostly spent with Norton waiting until Janis would relax her hold. Then he would quickly sneak into the back. Belle would panic. My mom would grab him. And he'd wind up back up front with Janis trying to convince him to stay put.

The second half hour was spent with Norton nestled on the ledge in the back seat. Belle saw how determined he was to get close to her so she agreed to let him sit nearby— as long as she didn't have to touch him. My mother kept a close eye on the cat, letting him get close but not *too* close.

An hour into the trip, we stopped for lunch at the Black Bass Inn in Bucks County, one of the great spots on the East Coast. It dates back to the 1700s and, except for the modernization of the dining room—picture windows that are both huge and a huge design error—the place still has the feel of a Revolutionary War tavern. It's right on the canal and, in the winter, scarf-wrapped kids skate by it on their way to another town, making you feel like you're about to bump into Loretta Young, Jimmy Gleason and Cary Grant as Dudley the angel in *The Bishop's Wife*. The five of us went in to eat. I noticed that things might be taking a turn for the better when Belle said that Norton could sit in the chair next to her. She gave an embarrassed little cough—in no way did she want to be seen as backing down—and muttered that he was so well behaved, what difference did it make where he sat.

Lunch was fairly uneventful—other than the fact that, somewhere toward the end of her meal, we all saw Belle sneak Norton a little piece of her chicken breast.

The last half hour of our car ride found Norton snuggled up next to Belle, taking up a third of the back seat. I'm sure my mother was a tad cramped back there, but I guess she knew that it was useless to complain.

The weekend we spent at Sweetwater Farm, in the town of Glen Mills, Pennsylvania, was absolutely spectacular. It was run by a couple named Rick and Grace. They had bought the spread, which included a gorgeous 1734 farmhouse and various outbuildings which they'd converted to extra rooms or suites. Rick was this handsome guy who seemed equally at home hunting or playing polo or making world-class breakfasts for the guests (a slightly intimidating combination, I must admit). Grace was the perfect hostess, quite warm and friendly, not to mention pretty. As a matter of fact, she looked a little like Grace Kelly, and there turned out to be a reason for that. The first night we were there, several of us—yes, including Norton—wandered into the den of the main house, where there were a pool table and bottles of brandy. My friend Ziggy (who, along with his wife, Nancy, were two of the regulars on the spring trips; one of the rules on these trips was "No Kids," so their son Charlie was left behind to fend for himself) decided we owed it to ourselves to sip and shoot, so we did, while Norton relaxed in a big, comfortable chair by the fireplace. In between shots, I couldn't help but notice that scattered all over the room were silver-framed photos of Grace Kelly—personal shots, not film stills. The next morning, I asked Rick what was up with that and he said that Grace Kelly was his wife Grace's aunt. This gave us an extra bond, since I'd always thought that I would have made a superb Prince of Monaco.

Norton, who would have made a superb Cat of Monaco, had come into contact with a variety of animals over the years—other cats, all shapes and sizes of dogs, a Vietnamese pig, a camel, even a wild boar. But he met his first goat and his first horse on this trip. The intro to the horse was relatively uneventful. Norton did some sniffing and then darted away, deciding there were far better ways of spending his time than hanging around with something a hundred times his size and one-tenth his intelligence. The meeting with the goat had a little more drama to it.

It turned out that Belle was not just afraid of cats. She was not thrilled with animals in general. So when she was strolling across the property, she did her best to ignore the shaggy-haired, white-gray goat that seemed intent on getting to know her. Being eighty, outrunning the beast was out of the question, so when the goat approached and nuzzled up to her, Belle did the natural thing. She held her hands out to keep him at bay. By the time I heard Belle's voice, calm but firm, saying, "Could someone come out here, please! Now!" what was happening was that the goat had his head down, Belle had her hands straight out in front of her, resting on the top of the goat's head, and the goat was slowly but surely pushing a little old lady across the lawn. You know how it looks when you run out of gas and you shift into neutral, have to put your shoulder down and try to push your car down the street? That's exactly what this reminded me of. Except in this instance, Belle was the car.

It wasn't all that difficult to disentangle her from her predicament, but I do have to say that the first person—well, the first, um, animal—on the scene was none other than Norton (this was several years ago and I was younger, but even then I did not possess catlike speed). Now, I will not go so far as to say that Norton was racing to rescue my aunt. Brilliant, yes, that I'd say about my cat. Fearless? Absolutely, certainly by normal cat standards. But having the instincts of a fireman, rushing off to save people at the drop of a hat? Uh-uh. I think, rather, he was simply fascinated by the sight (as were we all; there was a little difficulty on everyone's part trying not to laugh out loud as Belle was goat-skiing across the grass). When the goat saw Norton, he did turn his head, which gave Belle some breathing room. It's beyond my capabilities to imagine what the goat thought when he saw a cat running straight at him across the farmland. Nor can I picture the thought balloons above my Scottish Fold's head as he took in the image of his elderly traveling companion and the goat. I do know, however, that the standoff ended the crisis. A couple of us were able to push the goat toward some other distraction while Belle moved as quickly as it was possible for her to move back to her room and take a belt from the bottle of scotch secreted in her overnight bag. I also know that there were many other activities over those couple of days: a visit to the Hagley Museum in Wilmington, right across the river (the site of the original Du Pont mills, estate and gardens); Winterthur (one of those must-visit places in America; another Du Pont creation—majestic galleries of decorative art and early American furniture and a spectacular naturalistic garden); Longwood Gardens (Janis can never get enough garden-viewing into her life); and the ever-popular Mushroom Museum (Okay, this probably is not a must-visit place; take it up with Nancy Alderman, who on various trips with us has insisted we visit the Pencil Museum, the Coffee and Tea Museum and now, in Kennett Square, Pennsylvania, a place that revealed the fascinating history of fungi. In their brochure, they announce that you can "See the growing mushrooms in all stages of development" while you "discover the enchanting world of the Shiitake, Portabella, Crimini, and Oyster Mushrooms." There is also an "amazing array of distinctive gift ideas . . . all with mushroom motif." In case you doubt me, ask yourself this: Could he possibly make this stuff up?). But, by far, the best sight of all came in the car ride back to New York City. After spending a weekend with Norton—and surviving the harrowing run-in with the goat—Belle was more than happy to let my cat spend the ride sitting comfortably and purring away on her lap.

Living proof that it is never too late for an old dog— or human or cat—to learn new tricks.

In the wine country of Northern California, our friends Paul and Laurie Eagle "volunteered" to handle all the arrangements for the trip. And they did a superlative job, particularly in renting out three magnificent stone cottages on property belonging to one of the area's best wineries. It felt like we were sleeping in the middle of a vineyard in Tuscany. But as beautiful and as fun as this trip was, Norton was left behind (yes, he would have loved the vineyard accommodations; no, he would not have loved the Sarasota mud baths). I had one strict rule, which I always tried to adhere to when it came to Norton's travels. Flying is hard on a cat. Cross-country flying is harder (you try spending up to eight or ten hours—counting cab time to and from the airport—without your litter box). So unless I was going to be in California for at least a week, Norton would remain on his home coast. If he had seven days to relax and recuperate, I didn't mind dragging him along before putting him back on a plane. But even for the pleasure of his company, it wasn't fair to make him fly three thousand miles if it was only a two- or three-day trek.

Usually when I'd go away for under a week, it was for business, which meant that Janis would also be left behind and could take care of her step-cat. As is well documented, Norton was quite fond of Janis and nobody took better care of him. But as much as I hated being away from him, that's how much he did not like being separated from me. He was comfortable in Janis's apartment and got plenty of petting and friendly conversation as well as very acceptable sleeping arrangements (i.e., my side of the bed—or, in case that woman who wrote me the letter accusing me of moral degeneracy is actually reading this book, on the couch in the living room, where all male overnight visitors slept).

But when I'd call in from the road, here's the report I'd usually get:

Day One: Janis would report that all was fine. Norton slept next to her, tried to wake her up early so he could be fed (something he never did with me; but with Janis he would put his paw on her face and, at 6 A.M., he'd try to gently pry open her eyelids), and spent a peaceful day, moving around from room to room in her floor-through apartment.

Day Two: All was still fine, but Norton didn't do as much moving. He mostly napped in the foyer.

Day Three: Norton wouldn't look at Janis, clearly blaming her for my absence. He didn't sleep with her, either (too intimate, I guess, to sleep with such a traitor). Also, he was no longer relaxed and content. He was morose, hardly moving from the middle of the foyer. She did everything she could to coax him into her room but it was no go.

Day Four: Norton did nothing but sulk. Janis would use words like "clinical depression."

Day Five: He'd had it. Now furious that I was obviously having a good time without him, Norton would go into Janis's bedroom when she was away at her office and leave her a nasty little present. Right in the middle of her bed. Right on top of her antique linens and quilt. When Janis would return home, she'd call me, angry, sure, but also frustrated. "I treat him so well," she'd say. "I don't think it's right that he feels he has to shit in my bed."

I'd assure her that it wasn't personal and that I'd strongly reprimand my cat when I returned. But deep down, I was kind of glad. I certainly didn't wish a soiled quilt on anyone, particularly the love of my life. But if *I* was going to be depressed about being separated from my cat, it was comforting to know that he was just as neurotic as I was.

That San Francisco trip, he didn't stay with Janis, obviously, since she was there along with the rest of the usual group. For the three days we were gone, he stayed with a woman named Ann King. Weirdly enough, I hardly knew Ann. She was a close friend of a friend—and had gotten word to me that she was a huge fan of Norton's. The message was passed along that if the occasion ever arose, she'd love to take care of him (just so you know, *I* never get messages saying, "If you ever need someone to take care of you, just give me a call"). Since the occasion had arisen, I called her, asked if she'd like a cat for a long weekend and she jumped at the opportunity. When I dropped Norton off at her Chelsea apartment, he got his usual visiting-royalty treatment. Ann had special bowls all set up for his food and, while I stood by semi-invisibly, she showed her guest the entire apartment. By the time I left, Norton was happily exploring every nook and cranny. And when I returned to pick him up after the weekend, I got the full report: no depression, no morose sulking, no unpleasant surprises on the duvet cover. On both coasts, it was as successful a trip as it could have possibly been—except for Janis, who, deep down, was hoping that someone else would finally understand what she had to put up with.

The next spring, the destination was the Eastern Shore of Maryland. There was no cross-country traveling involved, so Norton was welcomed with open arms back into the group (Come on, admit it. Don't you think it's impressive that even after all these years I don't overdo the cute stuff and say things like "welcomed with open paws" in almost every paragraph?). I don't ever mean to make these books read like travelogues, but sometimes geographical description is truly in order. I'm also the kind of person who, when I like something a lot, I want everyone to like it as much as I do, so I generally do a lot of ranting and raving. And both Norton and I loved this part of Maryland.

First of all, what needs to be understood is that in Maryland, in the springtime, it is actually possible to eat all the hardshell crabs your little heart desires. And my heart desires a lot of those suckers. If you have never been fortunate enough to scarf some of these big boys down, what you do is go to a semi-divey-looking place with long wooden tables. The tables are usually covered with sheets of thick brown paper. As you sit and drink several pitchers of cold beer or, if you're the more delicate type, white wine, the servers bring out trays of hardshell crabs. Along with the crabs, you're given small wooden mallets (forks and knives are not just unnecessary, they're totally useless). These crabs are covered in the spiciest seasoning imaginable, red and peppery and so hot that I take pity on anyone who has a scratch on his fingers or who bites his cuticles because any exposed cut or wound will feel as if it's on fire. Before even trying to dig in, you get an explanation of how to eat them. Without this explanation, you're doomed to failure and frustration, because you'll wind up spending much money and getting about half an ounce of crab into you. If you follow directions—which involve expertly twisting various parts of the crab, delicately breaking parts in half, gently separating some parts from others, and then smashing down on everything as hard as you can with the mallet so you can get to the sweet, sweet meat—you will be rewarded with the perfect dinner. Most of the crab places I've been to down in those parts disdain vegetables as a side dish (another reason to love Maryland). And a lot of them serve brownies and ice cream with hot fudge for dessert. It's fairly heavenly, particularly if you're a cat. At the restaurant we went to, which was right on the water and glorious in its diveyness, Norton did not handle the mallet very well, but he was hell on wheels when it came to slurping up the crab I'd hand feed him (and if you're thinking of trying this at home, please do what I do: wipe off a lot of the hot stuff and get rid of the tiniest of bones before letting your cat attack it).

The town we decided to stay in was Chestertown and there are very few places like it left in America. It has a population of a little over three thousand and when you walk the streets it's like stepping back in time to the '70s. And not like stepping back to the 1970s. There are no platform shoes and discos here. I'm talking 1770s. The village is dominated by colonial and Victorian influences. If you go late at night or very early in the morning, when there are no cars driving around, stand in the middle of the bridge crossing the Chester River and turn back to Chestertown, you see absolutely no semblance of the modern world. It is not difficult to imagine Thomas Jefferson (or, if you're Norton, Thomas Jefferson's cat) strolling down High Street on his way to a town meeting (or prowling around looking for Betsy Ross's cat).

We stayed at a charming little hotel, which isn't difficult because everything in Chestertown is charming and little. Norton once again won the hotel workers over and spent much time lounging at the front desk. Our one big excursion was into Annapolis, which is the perfect southern seaport town—beautiful row houses, monied enough to be preserved but blue collar enough to be real. And it's got one of the great universities in the country, St. John's, which has one of the most interesting curriculums imagin-

able. Here's what you do in your four years at St. John's:
You read and study the hundred greatest books ever written. You get your basic Plutarch and Aristotle and
Archimedes and work your way forward to the twentieth
century. The brilliant idea behind it is that at the end of
your reading and discussions, you should have a decent
overview of what's made the world exactly what it is.

Sometimes—in fact, most of the time; more and more
of the time as I get older—I think that cats have a much
better idea than we do of exactly what the world really is.
They eat, they sleep, they choose who they love and bond
loyally. That's not a bad start. Add to it: They're not afraid
of being vulnerable, they are willing to please and to accept
pleasure with no questions asked. They are remarkably self-
sufficient, they are not obsessed with being liked, but they
will rarely, if ever, go out of their way to cause any sort of
pain or trauma. They are confident, with no need to show
it off, and they are kind, with little need of reward other
than to have that kindness returned.

I often wonder how different the world would be if
Plutarch and Aristotle and Archimedes had had cats.

A lot different, I think.

And I think this, too: a lot better.

CHAPTER 5

THE CAT WHO
WENT BACK
TO PARIS

N orton's travels were not confined to American shores. Whenever I was lucky enough to go to Europe, there was no question that he'd be lucky enough to accompany me. And just because he might not happen to speak the language of whichever country we were visiting, didn't mean that he couldn't change people's lives.

In Sicily, he totally and permanently transformed the lives of one of the most interesting and delightful families I've ever met.

Janis and I went to Sicily with Norton for the first time in 1991. Before we left—it was when we were living in Goult, that most heavenly of Provençal towns—our friend Nancy Alderman faxed us a small story about a restaurant called Gangivecchio, in the Madonie Mountains. It had my name all over it: it had originally been an abbey in the fourteenth century, it was in the middle of nowhere and impossible to find, and it supposedly had the best food in Sicily. Put all those things together and you've got this: Pete's goin' there to eat.

We started our Sicilian stay in the touristy but spectacular town Taormina (where Norton's adventures, particularly his tendency to scurry out on a ledge many hundreds of feet high, nearly giving his loving father a stroke, have been well chronicled). Our second day there, I insisted on trying to find the magical restaurant we'd read about, so we drove across a good chunk of the island to Gangivecchio. Or, rather, we *tried* to drive there. It was not as easy as it sounded (and it didn't sound all that easy to begin with). What should have taken two or two and a half hours, took four. Sicilian roads are small and if you're not inclined to blindly pass a slow-moving truck on a winding mountain road, you stand a good chance of driving along forever at twenty miles an hour. We didn't get stuck behind a truck— we got stuck behind *four* trucks. So we were not exactly speeding. And then we got lost (I'm not usually one to make excuses for my embarrassing and horrendous sense of direction—the only person I've ever met who can get more lost than I can is Janis—but the endgame of the directions included things like "When you come to a tree that branches off into a Y, across from a church, make a left"). Eventually we did find the place and it was magical indeed. Four hours of driving, squabbling and meowing were immediately forgotten.

A brief foray into seven hundred years of Gangivecchian history, because I think it's important to put Norton's influence into some kind of historical perspective:

In 1363, Benedictine monks were given a gift of 1,600 acres and began to build a priory on the spot of a village, Gangi, that no longer existed because it had been completely destroyed in a battle in the year 1299. The priory eventually became its own little village and I guess these monks knew what they were doing because at some point the priory had its designation elevated to "abbey."

Many fascinating things happened between that elevation in 1413 and the next 450 years—wars, invasions, religious upheaval, the usual sort of stuff—but the only real relevant item for our purposes is that in 1856, someone named Vincenzo Tornabene bought what was by then the *former* abbey (And just in case you don't think this book is educational, for all you historical dolts out there, 1856 was just five years before Sicily decided to unite with Italy. Tell the truth, you thought Sicily was *always* part of Italy, didn't you?). Various Tornabenes inherited the property over the next hundred years until Wanda Tornabene married the grandson of Vincenzo (whose name was also Vincenzo; trust me, I've spared you a *lot* of Tornabenes who all had the same name). Like many wealthy, land-owning Sicilians, Wanda's Vincenzo, who was called Enzo (I guess the Tornabene ancestors had the same problem I do telling everyone with the same name apart) found hard times after World War II. By the late 1970s, most of his money was gone, as were about 1,450 of the ex-abbey's acres and much of the magnificent furniture. That's when Wanda took over. They needed money, she had one great skill—cooking—so the abbey was now a restaurant. Life was not easy, but they survived—and managed to keep up the magnificent building and remaining property. By 1980, Wanda's cooking lured enough Sicilians so they had to expand the restaurant area and enclose an enormous second-floor terrace so it could function as a dining room. In 1984, Enzo died suddenly, but still the restaurant kept going, run by Wanda and her daughter, Giovanna.

And now we're in 1991. Enter three weary travelers: two humans and a cat.

Quite simply, after we finally arrived, we had the best lunch we'd ever had in our lives. If you want the actual details, we sat in the long room that had once been a terrace on the west wing of the abbey, looked out over the many acres of glorious wild red poppies, watched as various animals strolled nearby (including a pet wild boar) and ate the most amazing pasta with pesto sauce ever devised (one of several key secrets is the addition of five different kinds of crushed nuts: almonds, hazelnuts, walnuts, pistachios and pine nuts), veal rolls stuffed with ham (*"involtini"* is what you ask for, if you're ever lucky enough to make it there for lunch), *cannolis* that were not to be believed, and then something called *sofficini*, which you don't even want to know about because you might give up your life savings and your first born child in order to fly there and wrap your mouths around these things (Okay, I guess you *do* want to know about them, but don't say I didn't warn you: they're fried dough stuffed with warm lemon pastry cream. I guess I should mention that what adds to the taste, as well as the cholesterol level, is that they're not just fried, they're fried in lard. My fairly demanding friend and literary agent, Esther, has actually threatened to withhold payment of my next check that comes in from the publisher unless I learn to make these things and bring her some).

The restaurant was full that day—there were a hundred German bikers on a tour, which meant that every single person in the restaurant other than me and Janis was speaking German and wearing spandex—so we didn't get to talk very much to the two Tornabene women. The only reason they spoke to us at all was because Norton was fascinated with the place and, while we ate, he wandered the ancient abbey, exploring. At some point Wanda, the head of the family, came rushing over to us, muttering in Italian. My Italian basically consists of the following words (most of which I've already used in this chapter): *cannoli, pesto,* and *ciao bambino.* So I didn't really understand much of what Wanda was saying until Giovanna, who speaks lovely, charming, poetic English, also came over and said, "Mama is worried about your little cat." I told them both not to worry, searched for a minute, found Norton dozing on top of a table in some back room of this walled stone fortress, and convinced him that it was time to leave.

The next few days were spent touring the isle. I have absolutely nothing bad to say about Sicily. It's one of my favorite places on earth for many reasons—its beauty, its culture, its food, its relative wildness (as compared to, say, Tuscany, which Sicilians have mockingly labeled "Chiantishire" because it's been so Anglicized, or even to my beloved Provence which has been Peter Mayled to the point where it's almost easier to hear English spoken than French)—but the next few days were pure torture for me. I got crankier and crankier, and more and more impossible to be around, until Janis finally turned to me, while we were in front of the magnificent Greek temples of Agricento, one of the real wonders of the world, and said, "Why are you acting like a total asshole?!" Being the cultured guy that I am, I graciously answered, "Because I don't want to see any more temples, I don't want to go to any more museums, and I don't want to spend one more day being a damn tourist!" She calmly asked, as if talking to a petulant (if not very bright) sixth grader, "Well, then what *do* you want to do?" and I said, "I want to go back to Gangivecchio and eat!"

So the three of us got back in our rented car and drove three hours back to the abbey. Every so often we'd stop and try to call them, to make sure they were open, and we'd get some guy who answered the phone and said, "Pronto!" I'd then say, "Uh . . . openo for luncho?" and he'd hang up. Twenty minutes later, we'd call again, hoping to get Giovanna, the English speaker, but no, we'd get the same guy (we later learned his name was Pepe) who'd say, "Pronto!" I'd then say, "Uh . . . Giovanna?" And he'd say, "Si!" and still hang up. I called five times before we arrived, never managing to make Pepe understand a word I was saying, and when we finally showed up there wasn't a soul eating in the place. But Wanda and Giovanna let us in, served us an even more amazing lunch than we'd had five days earlier, and this time they both sat and chatted with us for several hours, Giovanna doing the translating all around. Norton sat with us for part of the time and spent the rest of the meal wandering around as if he'd spent his entire life there. Wanda, possibly the greatest animal lover I've ever met, was enthralled with my little guy and insisted on walking around with him and talking to him and feeding him.

At the end of the meal and quite a lot of conversation, when we realized we actually couldn't come up with an excuse to stick around one more moment, I said to Giovanna, "Would you like to do a cookbook? Because, if you would, I'll sign you up on the spot." (I worked then and still do work as an editor for various imprints within the humongous Random House Inc. complex, so I can do that sort of thing from time to time). They smiled, clearly thought I was trying to get a free meal out of them and said, "*Ciao*." I, however, wouldn't give up. When I got back to New York a couple of months later (remember, we were still living in France), I sent them a contract, found them a writer (a woman named Michele Evans, who'd written her own superb cookbooks and who heroically learned Italian for this job!) and we had a deal . . .

Sort of.

We didn't really have a deal because we'd hit one big snag. Wanda—the matriarch of the family and the one with all the recipes—didn't want to do it.

Two reasons. One: she didn't want her neighbors to be able to get their hands on her long-secret, much-valued family recipes. And two: she didn't know me from Adam and, being Sicilian, didn't exactly trust my motives. Why was I doing this? Why would I want to help them? What was I getting out of all this? etc., etc., etc.

Giovanna took care of Issue #1. She worked on her mother for weeks on end and Wanda began to weaken. I was able to push her over the edge by assuring her that the book would be published in English and none of her neighbors spoke anything but Italian, so her secrets would be safe.

Issue #2 was a little harder. What was there that could get her to trust me?

Well . . . there was one thing . . .

Norton.

After thinking and thinking, Wanda decided that anyone who traveled with his cat—and who loved his cat as much as I clearly did—had to be honorable. And anyone who had such a wonderful, brilliant, well-behaved cat, had to be a good person. Because she was so impressed with Norton, she thought there was a chance I just might be on the up and up. So she agreed to do the book. But she made it clear she was only doing it for Norton.

And thanks to Norton, here's what happened: The book was published in 1996. Giovanna and Wanda (who still didn't speak a word of English) went on a nationwide publicity tour in America and took the cooking world by storm. They went on television shows, including "Good Morning America"; cooked a magnificent lunch at the James Beard Foundation in Manhattan; were written about (gushed over is more like it) in just about every newspaper and magazine imaginable; and prepared special dinners at such famous restaurants as Alice Waters's Chez Panise in Berkeley and Mark Peel's and Nancy Silverton's Campanile in Los Angeles. As a result of all the publicity, the restaurant at the abbey in Gangivecchio was soon booked solid. Wanda's son Paolo, an architect, built a nine-room inn on the property (converting the old stables into lovely rooms and a separate dining room, for which he is now the chef). That inn is now always full. They also converted a two-hundred-year-old stone cottage into a luxurious two-room suite with an enormous stone fireplace in each room. To top it all off, their book won the James Beard Award as 1997's Best Italian Cookbook. Wanda and Giovanna Tornabene were officially stars. By the time you're reading this book in your hands, their second book will have been out for several months and will, I'm sure, be at least as successful as their first (and I do know that Wanda is now so proud of the first book, she even shows it off to her neighbors, recipe stealing be damned!).

It all makes for one of my favorite publishing stories. Lives were changed and totally for the better. And none of it would have happened if not for Norton.

Janis and Norton and I did go back to Gangivecchio a couple of years after the first book was published. We stayed at the inn this time and had a wonderful few days strolling the property and, of course, stuffing our faces (Wanda and Giovanna also took us shopping at the open-air food market in Palermo, a major treat). Norton had quite a good time, too. Not only was he fed well, he had 150 acres to stroll and many olive trees to climb and scratch. There were also a ton of animals on the property to keep him company. Paolo had a dog (a lunatic dog, but a dog), Wanda had her house dog, Puffo, and several indoor cats. Giovanna had her own dog, separate from Puffo, who was allowed indoors. And then there were quite a few outdoor dogs, whose favorite activity was to run up to us, barking as loud as they could, then stop short as soon as they saw an unfazed cat sitting on my shoulder and staring down at them. There was also that wild boar, who had his own penned-in area, but Norton, other than an occasional quick peek out of curiosity, tended to stay away from her.

When it was time to leave for the airport and return home, Norton was nowhere to be found. This was very unlike him. The door to our room had been left open, so I thought he was out strolling the property. I walked around calling his name, but got no response. This was now totally unlike him. My imagination ran somewhat wild. I had images of him being munched on by Wanda's boar. I had a vision of his being kidnapped by Sicilian bandits. I even thought that maybe Paolo had sent him to drive the car up to the house and boom!—blown to bits—but then I realized I'd just seen *Godfather II way* too many times. Finally, while standing in our room in the inn, wondering if I'd have to spend the rest of my life in Sicily searching for my cat, I heard a very familiar sound—purring. I searched everywhere and the purring got louder, but no Norton. Eventually, I put my ear to the bed and the purring got even louder. It turned out that Norton had crawled into and under the mattress cover. It was one of the very few times in his life he had tried hiding from me. I had to say, after two days of eating those lemon-filled *sofficini*, I couldn't blame him. But I picked him up (he'd gained a few pounds, just as his parents had), told him I didn't appreciate the anxiety he'd put me through, and did my best to convey the simple truism that all good things have to come to an end.

I don't know if I really convinced him, but he did let me place him in his travel Sherpa bag and we were finally able to return home.

To be honest, I don't think I really did convince him. That whole idea of good things ending was a concept Norton didn't fully understand and I can't say I blamed him. The truth is, I did my best to keep the good times rolling.

Some of the consistently best times were when we returned to France, particularly to Goult, which we tried to do once a year. We'd usually make an arrangement to rent the same house, because we loved it so much, then we'd go for Christmas and stay through New Year's Day, when all our Goultoise friends would have their traditional hike-into-the-hills-to-an-ancient-deserted-village-then-cook-homemade-sausages-over-an-open-fire-drink-wine-sing-songs-show-everyone-that-it's-much-better-to-be-French-than-anything-else celebration.

We actually mingled with two different crowds of people in Provence. There was the Goult crowd, mostly French with one Swede thrown in for good measure, and the ex-patriot crowd, mostly British with one or two Americans and Canadians. There was one Christmas party that was particularly memorable spent amongst the ex-pats. Our friends Margit and Georges decided to have a scavenger hunt. Well, Margit did. Georges, who's a bit more of the subtle, dry, academic type, went along with it. Margit, who's a bit more of the skin-tight pants, tight sweater, flamboyant, va-va-voom type, did all the planning and all the work. In addition to the va-va-voom, she's also been the CEO and CFO of various large companies, so it's not like this was a simple take-two-steps-due-east-of-the-well-until-you-find-a-tree-trunk kind of scavenger hunt. This was a major deal. After a wonderful lunch (did I mention that Margit is a serious cook, too?), we were divided into five different cars with four people—and in our case, one cat—in each car. Couples were split up, to make the whole thing more competitive. Margit didn't have to worry about the teams' competitive spirit, it turned out. By the end of the hunt, people were doing everything but letting the air out of enemy team car tires. Janis, at one point, threw herself down in the middle of the road so my team couldn't move our car—and thus get the jump on her team—without actually flattening her into a pancake. Or *crêpe*, as the case may be. What Margit did was give each team a set of extremely clever poems, some in French, some in English. The poems were complicated clues, each one leading us to find one element of the hunt. But you had to know this area well to figure things out. For instance, one particularly complicated segment of the poem wound up directing us toward the best bread baker in the region. Which meant we actually had to know who the best bread baker was. Whoever was smart enough to work it out, then had to buy one loaf of his particular specialty to prove that we'd concluded that segment of the hunt. My team figured it out, got to this *boulanger* first, but, being France, we got there during lunchtime when he was taking his nap. I was the one with the nerve to go wake him, and I also was the one with the nerve to suggest that he let me buy every single loaf of his special bread so no one else could possibly win. But this baker had too much integrity—or else he didn't understand my horrendous French—and he would sell me one loaf and one loaf only.

We spent the day racing all over what I think is the most beautiful region in the whole wide world. One clue led us up to the very top of the ancient village of Oppede-le-Vieux, where we had to find some hidden marbles. Another clue took us to an eighteenth-century fountain where we had to bring back a small container of water. We needed a handful of red clay from the magnificent village of Roussillon, too. I will admit that Norton was not a lot of help this particular day, although by his excited meowing, I do believe he got into the competitive spirit. Once all the clues were solved and the items collected, the final segment of the poem led us to one of my favorite places in the Luberon, the home of Gianni the Sardinian goatherd (who, as described in *A Cat Abroad*, had the unique arrangement of living with both his wife and his mistress). Gianni *et ses petites amies* lived on top of a mountain with hundreds of goats, some of whom were consumed nightly in the superb if extremely rustic restaurant Gianni had opened. So at the end of the big competition, the twenty or so humans and the one feline all wound up munching on roasted goat and delicious potatoes and drinking an obscene amount of Gianni's homemade (and devastating) *eau de vie*, all relishing our friendship and Margit's eccentric genius and the fact that a cat would actually spend the day helping to hunt for a perfect loaf of bread.

One year, I was lucky enough to stick around after the holidays. Norton and I spent two and a half months alone, ensconced in our house in Goult while I was working on a book. It was ten weeks of wine, cat and song, and just thinking of being able to live there makes me teary-eyed. I'd work all day, with a break or two to go grocery shopping at the mystical Madame Maurel's *épicerie*, where there was almost nothing on earth you wanted that you couldn't find. Norton would stroll down the cobblestone path, accompanying me daily to Joelle Maurel's store. He also liked to hike with me to the butcher shop. (Have you ever seen a cat lick his lips? I used to see it every day.) And to the *boulangerie*, where I'd get my daily bread. For those of you who have read the earlier books, you'll remember my good friend Norm Stiles, he of "Sesame Street" fame. (To refresh your memory, I wrote about how he used to lure babes over to the house we shared in Fire Island, shamelessly using any means possible, but I promised him I wouldn't bring that up anymore since he's now married. And you know me, I'm a man of my word.) Norm came to Goult several times and, in one sense, ruined my life. He used to do an impersonation of French people going through their daily lives and panicking when they realized they didn't have a loaf of bread under their arms. I used to go buy a baguette every single day in Goult and not once did I return to the house without laughing the entire way back, thinking of Norm going, in his horrendous French accent, "Ooh-la-la, I have no bread! If I don't get ze bread to tuck under my arm weezin fifteen minutes, I will be dead! Or worse, arrested by ze bread police!"

I never did figure out a way for Norton to carry his own baguette, which is one of the few regrets I have of time spent there. Other than that, the only word I can think of for Goult and its people and its shops is "perfect." There are many places in the world that I'm happy I've been to, and been able to take Norton to, but none quite so much as this Brigadoon-like town.

Janis and I felt extremely lucky that we were accepted so readily into this tight-knit Provençal society. And it was quite sweet to see the way Norton was accepted, too, just as if he were a full-fledged member of the family (which, of course, he was—but it was *très française* for the entire town to accept that fact so immediately and absolutely). Goult is tiny; there are perhaps a thousand people living there and we got to know many of them. One of the best and most interesting aspects of returning to the same place every year was that we could connect with our friends so strongly, even though we saw them but every twelve months or so. In a strange way, that separation added to the bond; it made our get-togethers more meaningful. And because we felt so close to them but were, in fact, so geographically distant, when we did reenter their lives we were able to clearly see how they and their surroundings had changed. Some changes were for the better, some weren't. I'm not big on change, in general. My succinct philosophy of life, stealing a line once written by Joseph Heller in his book *Good as Gold,* tends to be "All change is for the worse." But I will say that the changes in Goult were always fascinating.

We watched children grow up over the last decade and suddenly preteenagers who had once been shy around the American strangers were now our adult friends. We watched several women break up unhappy relationships with their husbands or male lovers and watched one of them, in quite a surprise move, take on a woman lover—and suddenly, for the first time in her life, have a genuinely good, mature relationship. She wrote to us before we arrived a few years ago, to try to prepare us for this change. Janis's French is better than mine, but neither of us are fluent. It's quite an experience trying to piece together a letter in French in which a friend is explaining that she's become a lesbian. After about seven or eight readings, we were pretty sure we'd narrowed things down. Either our good pal was now happily living with a woman and together they had a new dog called Yum-Yum. *Or* our friend was happily living with a gay dog who thought some woman was so delicious the dog was always saying yum-yum. (I made the case that, for all we knew, "yum-yum" was the French equivalent of "arf arf"). Or—this one was my interpretation—our friend was now convinced that she was a dog named Yum-Yum and she was living with another dog named Lesbian. We finally had to call another friend over there and gingerly ask, *"Qu'est-ce que c'est nouvelle avec notre amie?"* Our first interpretation was immediately confirmed, which, considering the possibilities, was quite a relief.

Over a decade of repeated visits, Janis, Norton and I

had witnessed close-up the ebb and flow of village life. One dear friend got so sick she almost died. Another was dying but made a miraculous recovery. One friend, a musician, moved to Paris and fell in love. Another returned from Paris to live in Goult full-time. Some of the Goultoise learned English since we'd first appeared. Some who spoke English forgot it. One woman sold her house and moved into the most beautiful eighteenth-century house imaginable. Another woman tried to sell her house but couldn't. Other friends built their dream house in the field right below the town.

And that was just on the human level. Norton experienced plenty of change, too. He found that some of his cat pals were no longer around—dead or just run away, no telling—but others replaced them, and as soon as he was back skulking in the lavender garden that comprised part of our backyard, many of the local *chats* would appear to play, hiss or scrounge food, depending on their moods. His bulldog pal, Archie, one of his favorite playmates, disappeared one year. No one in the town seemed to know what happened to him and I know that Norton missed him—he liked to explore the streets of Goult with Archie more than any of his other animal pals. But Norton definitely had a touch of French existentialism to him and he coped with Archie's absence quite well. One year here, the next year gone? *C'est la vie*. Time to move on . . .

No matter what the dramas or traumas, when we returned each year, everyone kissed us on the cheek—not just twice, three times is the rule in Provence—and we exchanged simple gifts and every single one of us thought how lucky we were to be together in such a magical and magnificent town.

My favorite change was pointed out to us one Christmas a couple of years ago. The three of us arrived late at night that year, driving up from the Marseille airport. One of the most startling things about Goult is how absolutely silent it is, especially when flying in from New York City, where silence is something that exists only in one's wildest imagination. Goult at 11 P.M. isn't just silent. It's as if you've suddenly gone deaf. There's not a noise to be heard. We parked toward the top of the village, behind the medieval castle, and walked down the hill, past the house that kept an outdoor canary cage, whose feathered inhabitants for some unknown reason never failed to terrify my heroic feline. Heading toward our house, our footsteps sounded to both of us like claps of thunder. We got the front door open and immediately felt a wave of pleasure sweep over us. The house, owned by a woman named Elisabeth Hopkins, is a special place both in reality and in our hearts, so we slowly and delightedly took it in, as we did every year. We looked to see which books on the shelves were new, if the furniture had been rearranged, if there were any new cooking utensils or sheets or decorations. Norton did what he always did, which never failed to amaze me: he went right for the exact spot where I put his food and water dishes every year and he just sat down, looking up at me expectantly. In case people ever say to you that cats don't have a real memory, ask them to explain how my cat could live in a house for a year, then return every twelve months for one week only, and remember, to the inch, exactly where he had to go for food.

Anyway, to finish off this little anecdote: After putting some French cat food right on Norton's marker, we unpacked, went into our cozy bedroom that had a window overlooking much of the glorious Luberon, and fell deep asleep. When we woke up the next morning, we strolled around town—which takes all of fifteen minutes—to see if we could ascertain what was new. The ruin at the very top of the town had been rebuilt and turned into a windmill, which it had apparently been many hundreds of years ago. There seemed to be a tiny new store that opened up (and when I say tiny, I mean *tiny*; the whole place couldn't have been any bigger than two subway token booths put together) although, since it was closed and all we could do was press our faces up against the window, we couldn't quite make out what it was they were selling. That seemed to be it. Everything else was pretty much the same.

So we thought.

At a respectable hour, we knocked on our friends Anne and Hannah's house (the nice thing about Goult is that no one lives more than about a hundred feet away from anyone else: Anne's house backed up onto our yard, Sylvie's house was ten feet away from Anne's on the other side of the street, Danie's house was fifteen feet away from our front door). Anne and Hannah let us in, made us some tea, put a bowl of water down for Norton, and then Anne went into a rant about how much Goult had changed.

"What's so different?" I asked, a bit bewildered by the tirade.

I was almost sorry I asked. There used to be *two* restaurants in town—now there were *three* (when we started going there, there was only one restaurant, but we didn't want to remind her of that)! Patrick, the owner of the first restaurant, Le Tonneau, had opened a bed-and-breakfast above his bistro! And worst of all, the new store we'd seen in the middle of town, well it wasn't a new store, it was a small tourist agency. Tourists could go there and send faxes or ask about tour guides or . . . or . . . or . . . Anne could barely finish she was so upset.

"Goult, eet ees just like Shee-cago!" she said despairingly.

We tried to explain to her that three tourists showing up there so they could buy a map wasn't exactly like Chicago, but it was no go. She could not be convinced.

"Perspective," I said to Norton when we got home. He was sitting on the tiled roof of the house, outside our living room window, his favorite perch. "Don't ever lose it," I told him.

Watching him lolling in the Provençal sun, staring out at the hills of the Luberon, I had the comforting feeling that Norton's perspective was one thing I didn't have to worry about changing.

Most of the time, when we returned to Goult at Christmastime, we tried to spend a day or two in Paris. Janis and I love Paris, and always have had a perfect time there, but nobody has ever liked it as much as Norton.

When we'd hit the City of Lights, he went everywhere with us: to breakfast, to lunch, to dinner, out wandering the streets. People often stopped to chat with him and he was even recognized a few times. In restaurants he'd be wined and dined (or, to be more accurate, milked and dined), and he was always ready to make himself at home in any of the perfectly groomed parks or pet-friendly cafes.

Once, Janis and I went to do some shopping along *rue Jacob* and up and down all the little streets in the sixth *ar-*

rondissement that are littered with antique shops, and we decided to split up (cleverly hoping to find last-minute Christmas gifts for each other). Naturally, Norton went with me, comfortably ensconced in his shoulder bag. We popped in and out of a few stores, then came to one that I particularly liked and had frequented over the years. Cat and I stepped inside, not only because this woman had beautiful things but because she was very friendly and, over the years, whenever she would see me she would speak French slowly enough so we could have a semireal conversation. I liked nothing better than pretending I actually spoke French and she was nice enough to encourage my fantasy. I remembered that the last time I'd popped in, I told her that we had lived in Goult and she knew the town well, she'd had relatives who lived nearby. So this time, when she saw me, her eyes lit up. (While I do harbor fantasies about speaking the language, I don't harbor fantasies about why she remembered me; I was clearly the only person who regularly shopped in her boutique with a cat on his shoulder.) She got all excited and told me that she'd gone out and bought the French edition of *The Cat Who Went to Paris* after our last conversation. As excited as she normally was to see Norton, now she was doubly thrilled. We spent a few minutes chatting, while she petted the cat. She asked me if certain things had really happened the way I'd described them in the book (they had) and if Norton had really done some of the things I'd said he'd done (he definitely had) and then she noticed that, even as we carried on our conversation, I was staring off to the side and behind her, at the most beautiful antique desk I'd ever laid eyes on. It was late eighteenth century and I'm absolutely terrible at describing furniture because I wind up saying things like, "Well, you know, the front folded down and it was hand carved and the legs were kind of spindly," and no matter how beautiful the object is, I make it sound like the desk I had in my third-grade class. But this desk was spectacular and I'll leave it at that. It was so spectacular that I decided I'd do almost anything to own it, then realized I'd have to relegate this to another one of my fantasies, because when I checked the price tag, the thing cost about twenty thousand dollars. Instead of buying, I drooled and got the store owner to tell me a little bit about the desk's history, then before long, another man had come into the store because he'd spotted the desk from the street and wanted to get a closer look. The four of us—two men, a woman and a cat—stood before the desk admiringly and talked for about fifteen minutes. It was fairly obvious to me that this man wasn't only fantasizing; I got the distinct impression he could, at any moment, reach into his pocket and pay for this baby in cold, hard francs.

But he was quite nice and, after he'd gotten all the information he wanted about *l'objet ancienne*, he turned his attention to you-know-who.

"That is a very handsome cat," he told me in French ("*Le chat, il est très, très beau*," is how it came out). I nodded and smiled.

Then he said, sizing Norton up, "*Et très sage*." That means, "And quite well behaved." For years, I thought that "*sage*" meant "wise," so I gloated in *A Cat Abroad* that so many French people understood how brilliant Norton was, how truly existential. About a billion readers immediately wrote to me to explain that when referring to animals, "*sage*" actually means "calm" or "well-behaved." Another illusion shattered—and rather publicly, too—but the way this man said it, it still sounded pretty damn good.

"*Oui*," I said, showing him that even if at one point in my life I didn't know what *"sage"* meant, I could *parlez* a little *français*, and I thanked him again.

Then this man, who I noticed was about sixty or sixty-five and incredibly handsome—he had that air of sophistication, that certain *je ne sais quoi*, as if he could walk for hundreds of miles with his jacket draped casually over his shoulders and never let it fall; I do not have quite that same air, since I can't even get through a meal without spilling most of my food all over my shirt—said, "*Et il est très sophistiqué.*"

"Yes," I said, "he is very sophisticated."

The woman who owned the store proceeded to tell this very charming gentleman all about my cat and his travels and how he was a famous literary cat. The man smiled, duly impressed, asked something more about the desk, said he'd be back, then turned and sauntered out.

I turned to say something to the woman but she had a dreamy, faraway look in her eyes and she sighed, "*Je lui adore*" ("I love him." But it came out more like, "I loooovvve him"). I nodded politely, and when she saw the blank look in my eyes, she said, "Don't you know who that is?"

Okay, I have to interrupt now. I have this fatal flaw. Well, I don't know if it's fatal, but it's definitely embarrassing. My problem is that I don't recognize *anyone*. I mean nobody! If I see someone out of context, I don't have a clue. To show you how bad it is, several years ago I had a meeting with an actor. We spent about forty-five minutes together in my office, hit it off fine, and that was that—except that Janis, who then had an office right near mine, was absolutely livid that I hadn't introduced her (as, by the way, was every woman at the company). Two days after the meeting (and a day after Janis stopped yelling at me) we had to go to L.A. for business. We were staying at The Four Seasons, as usual, and we got in the elevator to go down to the lobby. The elevator stopped a floor below ours and someone stepped in. Janis stared at him for a moment, then said, "Oh, I believe you two know each other." The guy looked at me, smiled, and said, "Peter, what are you doing here?" I looked at him with absolutely no recognition, until he finally realized I didn't have a clue who he was. It turned out he was the actor I'd met with in my office, and he said, "It's me. Mel . . . *Mel Gibson.*"

Needless to say, Janis wanted to murder me. But the truth is, there's actually some part of my brain that just can't recognize people or remember their names. No matter who they are. Part of it, I suppose, is that I tend to concentrate on things other than facial features. I remember once waiting in line for a movie on the Upper East Side and saying to my date that night, "Wow! Do you see that guy with the worst toupee in the world?" I also remember her saying, "Do you mean Sir John Gielgud?"

Anyway . . .

I clearly had one of those mental blocks in Paris because when the store owner stared at me incredulously and said, "Don't you know who that is?" I said, "No," and she shook her head and said, "Marcello Mastroianni!"

What made this so pathetic is that Marcello Mastroianni is in my top ten list of favorite actors of all time. Every eighteen months or so I watch *La Dolce Vita*, which probably gets my vote as the greatest movie ever made, to chart my mental health. If I get overwhelmingly depressed, as is usually the case when the film's over since it's the most devastatingly depressing movie imaginable, I figure I'm pretty much on top of things. So before my favorite shop owner could find me any more pitiful than she already did, I dashed out to the street—Norton swinging wildly on my shoulder—and ran until I could catch up to the guy from the shop. I sped about twenty steps past him, then turned and, trying to be cool, walked back the way I'd come, right by him, staring at his face. Sure enough, it was Fellini's favorite actor. And sure enough, he recognized me, too. How could he not, since I was the same guy he'd seen just seconds before, standing in the store chatting casually with a cat on my shoulder.

I didn't speak to him as we passed, I merely ascertained that he was who he was supposed to be, but I've always wondered what he thought when he saw us. Did he wonder how in hell I'd managed to get there and be heading in the wrong direction so quickly? Or *why* in hell I'd managed to get there and be heading in the wrong direction?

Or did he wonder if there were *two* bearded Americans strolling the streets of Paris with very, very wise, well-behaved and sophisticated cats on their shoulders . . .

CHAPTER 6

A CAT IN RETIREMENT

I don't spend nearly as much time in Europe as I'd like to, or as I think is necessary to keep a civilized and centered point of view. One of the reasons is that there's a town in Long Island which I think of as my American Goult, and that's the town of Sag Harbor.

Sag Harbor is on the north side of the South Fork of Long Island, one hundred miles and a two-hour drive from New York City, except on Fridays during the summer when, thanks to all the traffic heading out toward the beach, it's about a twelve-hour drive.

I hate to sound like Andy Rooney, but like just about everything else in the world, Sag Harbor isn't what it was twenty years ago (reminds you of my motto, doesn't it: All Change Is for the Worse). There are housing developments and lots of traffic now. It's not as quaint as it used to be, it's not as quiet, many of the small town businesses have been replaced by upscale restaurants and tourist (i.e., expensive) shops, and there are too many Hollywood-type people who come east for the summer and can be seen dining and strolling and just generally being repulsive. What's happened to Sag Harbor is that it has become "Hamptonized" due to its proximity to the more glamorous (i.e., *very* expensive) towns of East Hampton, Bridgehampton and Southhampton. All that said, however, it's still a wonderful and special place and it's still got more charm and quaintness and more of a small town feel than most places within a reasonable drive of Manhattan. Lillian, the woman who runs the fish store, lets me sign for my fresh tuna and lobster and sea bass and bills me whenever she gets around to it; Linda Sylvester, who runs the cleverly named and very hip general store Sylvester's, will often give me a cup of hot coffee on a blustery winter day if I show up looking properly bedraggled; at Christmastime there's always a house tour of some of the two-hundred-year-old houses, where they serve little cups of eggnog with Christmas cookies; and the movie theater on Main Street still serves grape drink out of one of those waterfall-looking clear canisters and looks as if Glenn Ford should still be headlining whatever's playing there. I love Sag Harbor and I will love it forever and that's all there is to it.

Norton is largely responsible for my having moved to Sag Harbor and I'd say that his attachment to the place has been just as profound as mine. In fact, there are many parallels when comparing our two existences in our hometown away from hometown.

Norton is not normally an overly social cat, although he learned to tolerate and even enjoy public life. In private, he is perfectly friendly and rarely gets his hackles up, but he is fairly blasé when it comes to reaching out for affection, both with humans and with animals of the four-legged variety. He can, for the most part, take or leave other cats who have on occasion tried to be friendly; he can take or leave the big dogs who from time to time have come into his life; and he can pretty much leave the tiny, yippy dogs who have hopped and barked around him during his normal naptime. But in Sag Harbor, when Norton was about thirteen years old, this little black female kitten kept coming into our yard looking for a playmate. At first Norton, noted macho poseur, would hiss at her and make it clear that playful, youthful kittens were not a welcome addition to his ever more sentient life. But the kitten would not take no for an answer. After several weeks of repeated visits, the hissing stopped and Norton went through his I'll-tolerate-this-but-I-won't-get-too-involved period. That was fine with the kitten, who would run around while Norton sat and watched. Occasionally this black cat would force Norton to move or wrestle or join in a brief hunt for a butterfly that might be fluttering around. Within another few weeks, Norton did not have to be forced to do anything. The kitten had my elder statesman frolicking like a . . . well . . . like a kitten. His new ebony friend would show up every day (to this day I don't know where she came from) hang out in the yard, run around with Norton, and then nestle up close to him and relax in the sun. I think Norton liked this mentoring process because I'd often spot him licking the kitten (cleaning her, I assume, since any other possible urges had long ago been snipped away) or nudging her into more comfortable napping spots on our brick patio. I quite liked to watch this because if I ever felt guilty about anything that I'd ever done—or not done—with my cat it's that I was too selfish to get a second cat for him to socialize with. I always thought that as Norton got older, slowed down, and spent less time traveling and more time at home, I'd get him a companion. That way, if I left for a few days, he'd have some company he could relate to. And, just possibly, he'd stop relieving himself on Janis's bed come Day Five of my absence (of course, the other, more horrible alternative, would be that Janis would have *two* cats taking a dump on her bed; but I didn't even want to think about that possibility). Over the years, however, I never acted on my initial impulse. If you really want to know, I valued my companionship with Norton so much that I really didn't want anything to interfere with that. Yes, I realize that it sounds slightly crazy to think of being jealous of a second cat, but I would have been. I also believe that Norton felt the same way. I knew I couldn't travel with two cats, and I decided that Norton would prefer being with me than hanging out at the ol' homestead with another feline. Our bond, I decided, was stronger than any transpecies relationships that might be needed. But our little black kitten neighbor took care of all my worries. I didn't have to get another cat and Norton had a regular playmate to do the things I would normally pass on—in particular, mousing, butterfly chasing and tree climbing.

I went through a similar process of finding my own play dates in Sag Harbor.

Ever since we returned from Provence, I've spent the entire summer, from June until the end of September, out at my Long Island hideaway, venturing into the city only when absolutely necessary. I do it for several reasons. One, it's a wonderful place for me to work. My office overlooks our beautiful garden (which Janis is totally responsible for, other than my yearly contribution of whining like crazy then working the back forty—or, in our case, back one-third of an acre—to plant several billion tulip bulbs, usually in the pouring rain) and I very much enjoy spending hour upon hour in there hunched over my computer. Two, I can actually be alone out there, or rather, without *human* companionship, and that's something I greatly value. New York City is a social place and my publishing job is a particularly social one. The good part of that is that I get to take writers and agents and almost anyone I find interesting to excellent restaurants. The bad part is that most writers and agents can be major pains in the ass and most people I expect to be interesting turn out to be fairly boring because they mostly like to talk about themselves. The writing part of my life is also fairly social, at least in the city, because it involves sucking up to studio and television executives or, to be more precise, to New York studio and television executives, who are even lower on the evolutionary scale than their California counterparts because, for the most part, if they were any good at all they'd be in L.A. The bottom line is that, if left to my absolute druthers, I'd basically be a hermit. And Sag Harbor lets me pretend, albeit for just a portion of the year, that I can get away from it all.

The first few years I spent my summer there, this was my routine: wake up, run a mile or two, have a little breakfast, work all day, have dinner (way too often pizza and beer). When the wonderful invention known as DIRECTTV came along and I added a tiny satellite to our roof, I could add to that list: watch sports or movies all night long. I didn't have to talk, I didn't have to be friendly,

I didn't have to do anything for anybody (except for Thursday nights through Monday mornings, when Janis would appear and then I would willingly enter civilization). I could, when work was done, eat, drink and vegetate. On the occasions when Norton would actually deign to eat pizza, we had become true soulmates.

The longer this went on, the more I liked the routine. And then I found out I was not alone. There were a lot of women who did the same thing I did (except mostly without the beer and pizza). Their husbands would arrive in Long Island Thursday nights or Friday afternoons, spend the weekend, then the wives would drive them to the train station on Monday morning, kiss 'em goodbye, and return to their weekday existence of self-sufficiency (and, rather than taking care of a cat, taking care of a child or two or three). I realized that every Monday morn, there I'd be, waving goodbye to Janis at the Bridgehampton train station, standing among a hundred women waving goodbye to their husbands. When the train took off, I'd look around and I'd see many of those women staring at me. I had a feeling quite a few of them were thinking, *Oh, what a sensitive guy. He must be a househusband, taking care of the kids.* I toyed with the idea of having a placard made explaining that I wasn't really so sensitive and that I was actually a cathusband, but I decided I was better off keeping quiet.

On the weekends, I'd discuss this phenomenon with various friends who had houses out there, particularly those friends who were in my exact same position. There were three couples we saw regularly in the summer months: Nancy and Ziggy, who have already been dissected in previous Norton books (You might remember that Ziggy is also known by various other names at his place of employment. Some people know him as John, some as Jack, quite a few refer to him as Aldy, and now, in his latest Wall Street incarnation, he apparently has become Old John, because his new assistant has become Young John), Ed and Caroline, and Tom and Andi. During those months, Ziggy, Ed and Tom would head back to the city every Monday morn, grumbling about my life of ease, while Nancy, Caroline and Andi would remain behind, wondering what I was actually doing all by myself in my little Victorian house. Over a period of weeks, our conversations progressed much like Norton's sparring with his kitten pal. First we'd talk about how lucky we were to be able to stay in Long Island for such a long time. Then we'd talk about how we valued the time alone (or with cat/children). Then we'd say things like, "You know, why don't we all go to a movie on Wednesday night?" Once we did that, it became, "Why don't we go to a movie *every* Wednesday night," and the next thing I knew I was having a Girls' Night Out once a week. Nancy, Caroline, Andy and I (along with a rotating group of women who would be out in our neck of the woods for this auspicious occasion) would head out to a flick, have dinner and catch up on all the typical gal stuff. I'd hear about their kids' soccer games, they'd hear about the latest blue jay who tried to peck Norton on the head. They'd try to get me to drink white wine, I'd see if I could turn them on to the joys of martinis and surf 'n' turf. They'd listen to a little Mets stuff without squirming too much, I'd do my best to listen to something that had to do with women's bodily functions without passing out. All in all, it became a night out on the town that we all looked forward to.

We looked forward to it so much that GNO—as it came to be called—carried over to the next summer. And the next and the next and so on. It became such a popular event that eventually we all got laminated membership cards, legitimizing the group (and detailing the strict guidelines for inclusion, the key being that you can pay for dinner when needed). It also caused a little jealousy among spouses who, when we were all together, wanted to know why they were never invited to our other get-togethers. We'd try to explain that it was girls only—and then I'd realize that everyone would be staring at me and all I could do was smile and shrug and hope no one would spend too much time thinking about it. Especially Janis.

There were a few awkward moments that arose from time to time, I must admit.

Nancy and Ziggy's son, Charlie, also spent the summer out in Sag Harbor and Charlie is, to say the least, a precocious lad. The little bugger doesn't miss a trick or forget a thing. We're also pretty good pals. Now that he's close to his teenage years, he's got the freedom to ride his bike over to my place, which he will do on occasion so we can talk sports or Adam Sandler movies, two passions we both share. He's also obsessed with wanting to see a movie that has naked women in it, which gives us another common passion. Every so often, particularly when he was younger, around eight or nine, I'd go over to pick up his mom for our dinner and I'd get grilled by the Chuckster. A typical conversation would be:

Charlie: Hey, Pete. What's up?
Me: Big night tonight. Dinner and a movie.
Charlie: Girls' Night Out?

Me: Yup.
Charlie: (with furrowed brow and look of great confusion):
    Can I ask you a question?
Me: Sure.
Charlie: Isn't Girls' Night Out for girls?
Me: You bet.
Charlie (after a long silence and a *lot* more furrowing): Have
    a good time.

Once, in my second or third summer of GNOing, Janis
and I were having dinner with two friends, Oren and Betsy
(I had to be in the city that day, briefly breaking my summer isolation). During the course of dinner, Betsy started
hemming and hawing and finally said, "I was talking to
Andi on the phone a few days ago and she was all excited
because she said she was going to Girls' Night Out that
night. She told me how much she looks forward to it and
she was explaining that all her women pals out there go out
and eat and drink and talk . . ."

She kind of drifted off uncomfortably, then Oren
nudged her so she went on: "Uh . . . I asked her who went
and she said Nancy, Caroline, that night Esther was going . . . and . . . uh . . . you."

I nodded and went on eating. Betsy waited politely for
another few seconds then quietly said, "Um . . . is there
anything you want to tell us?"

When I assured her there wasn't, she and Oren resumed eating—and thinking God only knows what.

My cat's life and mine were comparable, too, in ways
other than establishing stimulating, platonic relationships
with members of the opposite sex out there in summery
Sag Harbor.

I wasn't much for skulking through the high grass of our backyard looking for little critters. But I could regularly be found skulking through the fescue of a nearby golf course looking for lost little white balls.

At the end of a tough day in the sunshine, Norton liked nothing better than to chew on a bit of catnip, collapse on the couch in the den and relax. After a tough day in my upstairs office, I liked nothing better than to gulp down a Pete's Wicked Ale, collapse on the same couch and watch any movie that might be on the satellite system that had Greta Scacchi in it (here's an in-print promise to my now twelve-year-old pal, Charlie: when your mom says you're old enough, you can come over and we can watch *White Mischief* together).

Come the late afternoon, Norton liked to clamber up onto my desk to get his ears and stomach scratched and rubbed for quite a long while.

I found out that one could actually get masseuses to work at one's house, so come the late afternoon I would, on occasion, find myself on a massage table in the backyard, listening to Miles Davis or Chet Baker, getting my ears, stomach and just about every other part of my body rubbed.

But we weren't just slugs, Norton and I. For one thing, we did quite a bit of work.

I wrote books and television shows and the occasional movie.

And, after a few years of having nothing to do with the literary community, Norton wrote his own book.

Well, let me elaborate on that.

I'm very grateful to everyone who reads these Norton books (actually, I'm more grateful to those who buy them, but reading them is okay, too). Clearly, anyone who reads hundreds of pages about the adventures of a nine-pound, four-legged creature with folded ears can be legitimately described as a "cat lunatic." Just as clearly, there is a reason why the phrase "cat lunatic" has the word "lunatic" in it. I speak from experience. Not that long ago, my agent, Esther Newberg, called because she was a little depressed. She had just gotten a gift from a friend—a beautiful frame, and inside it was a photo of Esther's cat, Tate. Esther thought it was a tad weird to realize that, as symbolized by the friend's choice of photographic subject, the closest relationship in her life was with a feline. I had to interrupt her and point out that all she had was one little photo of her cat. I'd spent the last decade of my life writing entire *books* about my relationship with my cat. And going around the world talking about him. "*Weird*?" I said. "Forget just being my best friend, my cat also *supports* me!" She agreed that I topped her in the "weird" category.

The point is, I have pretty good anecdotal proof by this time that just about *every* cat person should have the word "lunatic" attached to his or her name as a permanent appendage. But my fans do seem to take it to new heights. So when my good friend Norm Stiles and I dashed off what we thought was the world's funniest book, *Historical Cats*, and put on the cover that it was written by Norton, I have this sneaking suspicion that way too many of my readers went, "Oh, okay, well he *is* a genius cat, I guess he *could* have written it." You'd be amazed, when Norton and I went back on tour to promote this book, how many people asked, at the readings, "So how much did Norton actually contribute to the book?" I would answer, as seriously as I could manage, that the idea was his, that he did the research and chose which cats to use, and that Norm and I only helped him with the jokes. You'd be more amazed if I told you how many heads would nod after that, the look in their eyes saying, "Yeah, that's pretty much what I thought."

Now, I'm not saying he didn't have *anything* to do with the writing of the book. Of course he did. The premise of *Historical Cats* was that, as all of us lunatics know, behind every great human there is an even greater cat. So we imagined various figures throughout history and came up with what we thought was a realistic portrait of that person's lesser known feline companion (and got a brilliant illustrator, William Bramhall, to bring those portraits to life). For instance, there was that great American patriot, Nathan Hale's cat, who uttered the immortal words, "I regret that I have but nine lives to give for my country." And, of course, there was Marie Antoinette's cat, whose dismissive *bon mot* to the French peasants was, "Let them eat dry food." And, among many, many others, was JFK's cat, whose most inspirational rallying cry was, "Ask not what you can do for your human, ask what your human can do for you." Officially, for the record, Norton did not write these. He did use his discerning taste to help, though. While sitting around Norm's house listening to the two of us making each other laugh, Norton would occasionally close the pages of one of our history books or encyclopedias, basically saying, "Nice try, boys, but come up with something better."

And, so I don't shatter every one of his fan's illusions, he *did* write the introduction to the book, which I will reprint here:

INTRODUCTION
by NORTON, The Cat Who Went to Paris

This was not an easy book to write. Let's face it—
no book is easy to write when you don't have opposable thumbs.

Living in semiretirement after my last book
tour, I suppose I could have been content to spend
the rest of my nine lives in the lap of luxury (and I
mean that literally; my human has a very comfortable lap). However, on my many travels throughout the world, I did not merely dine out in fancy
restaurants and act cute on airplanes, despite the
distortions written about me by my so-called
owner in *The Cat Who Went to Paris* and *A Cat
Abroad*. In my free time, I didn't just curl up *on* a
few books, I curled up *with* a few good books. And
what I read really began to make my fur stand on
end. Ever since I was a kitten riding around town
in my human's pocket, I was a history buff. Now,
as I began to leap up onto library shelves in search
of feline facts, I found a void. A wasteland. An endless litter box in which the history of an entire
species seemed to be buried.

While there are countless numbers of books on
Thomas Jefferson, where is the book on Thomas
Jefferson's cat? Why are his once magnificent catnip
gardens no longer found at Monticello? And where
do you think Jefferson got the idea for independence in the first place? While we're on the subject,
how is it possible that so little is known about Søren
Kierkegaard's cat, who developed the brilliant phi-

losophy that all dogs are merely a figment of the imagination? Why is there no monument to Ernest Hemingway's cat, who wrote the classic *A Farewell to Mice*? Or to Joe DiMaggio's cat, who not only ate chicken in gravy fifty-six days in a row, but was married to Marilyn Monroe's cat? The answer, my friends, is *catism*. But the fact that cats have been at the center of all historical events since the beginning of time—remember Adam and Eve's cat, Ribs?—is a secret that can no longer be kept. *Must* no longer be kept.

Thus this book. My collaborators and I have attempted to right the wrongs of history. We have scoured the world in search of rare manuscripts; we have conducted thousands of interviews and skritched hundreds of bellies in an attempt to get information. I apologize for any omissions, but if there are any errors, I can only claim *meow culpa*. If it is true that behind every great man there is a great woman, then it is even truer that behind every great human there is an even greater cat. I just hope that our research and our passion can, at long last, bring that fact forth to the world at large.

—NORTON
Sag Harbor, New York

I have to say, reading that over these several years later, I'm impressed yet again by how eloquent my cat can be, especially considering that English is not his first language. Of course, I shudder to think what that would have read like if it had *been* in his first language. But I'll leave that to the scholars. Maybe Vladimir Nabokov's cat . . .

Although there was this brief foray back into the working world, Norton and I mostly stayed out of the public eye during this period. Of course, with Norton around it was impossible to stay totally away from the social scene. He was too much in demand.

He not only attended any and all dinner parties that Janis and I threw, he was often invited to come along to some of the parties we were invited to. If we'd stroll down to the Halloween parade in town (featuring just about every kid on the east end of Long Island), Norton would stroll along with us. If we went to a friend's house to swim or have brunch, Norton would happily attend—he didn't swim but he was a good sunbather, and he brunched extremely well. If friends gathered, Norton could usually be found gathering as well, and almost always enjoying it. I say "almost" because I have to include the time when we met up with friends Ed and Caroline and their kids to exchange Christmas gifts. One of their gifts was for Norton—an angel costume. We did put the little halo, as well as the translucent white wings, on my cat to see how he'd look. I suppose I have to say he didn't look too good since it took Ed and Caroline a while to convince me that it wasn't actually a reindeer costume. Norton didn't seem too impressed with this form of dress-up, either. I can honestly report that this was a gathering he was not wild about.

One of our weirdest social engagements started as a result of a Sunday brunch with Nancy and Ziggy. When we were seated and about to dip into our scrambled eggs, Zig announced that he had a little story to relate. He then proceeded to tell us about something that had happened to him the night before. He and Nancy had to go to some fancy business party. You know, one of those go-to-a-billionaire's-oceanfront-mansion-with-a-huge-tent-that-holds-two-hundred-people-on-the-lawn-and-live-entertainment-by-somebody-you've-actually-heard-of-like-Gladys-Knight-type of affairs that we all frequent on a regular basis. They had to go because this particular billionaire was one of Ziggy's clients. While there, Ziggy found that his dinner partner was a woman who absolutely terrified him. He described her as the scariest person on Wall Street: tough, brutal, merciless when it came to making money. Ziggy, who's never intimidated by anything, was totally intimidated by her. But he decided, this Saturday night, with some prompting from Nancy, to speak to this woman and to get over his fear and intimidation.

Okay . . . dinner's served, they sit down. Zig bobs his head up and down several hundred times and smiles, trying to think of something to say that won't make him sound like a total moron. They chat about business things for a while, he manages not to put his foot in his mouth. Then, for some reason, someone at the table says something about dogs. The Bride of Frankenstein perks up a bit and asks Ziggy if he's got a dog. He says no. Then he says, for absolutely no reason, "I have a friend with a cat, though." She looks at him like he's lost his mind, which he's beginning to think he has. He wants to say, "Oh, forget I said anything and let's just go back to talking about your money!" but he's stuck with this topic for a while, so he goes about the process of digging himself in deeper and deeper. "My friend really loves his cat," Zig now says, starting to sweat a little bit as the rest of the table stares at him blankly. And then, to finish things off and seal his doom, he mutters, "He even wrote a book about the cat."

At this point, the Scariest Woman in the World jerks her head up, stares right at Ziggy and says, in as excited a tone as if he'd just told her that IBM went up a hundred points, "Is his cat named Norton?"

My buddy Zig almost fell over backward in his chair. And the whole thing got weirder and weirder as the New York winner of the Miss Terrifying contest then began to plead with him, begging him for an introduction to my cat.

At the brunch table, our eggs were now cold. Janis was shaking her head in that I-can't-believe-this-is-happening-again kind of way, and Ziggy finally turned to me and said, "So . . . um . . . do you think Norton could pay a visit to my client?" He went on to explain that it would be a major career boost, that it could really help him in the future, that she was his most important client, etc., etc., etc.

As much as I loved the groveling, I finally told him I didn't see any problem. Scottish Folds are known for always wanting to help out their buddies, I said, so after the dishes were cleared away, Zig called the woman, said that Norton would be thrilled to come a calling later that afternoon, and then he reported back to us that he'd never heard anyone quite so excited in his entire life.

A few hours later, Zig drove by and picked us up. Norton was in his Sunday best—which was actually the same as his Monday through Saturday best, but he did look particularly spiffy—and then we drove into Bridgehampton until we got to a very large, very new, slightly terrifying house on the beach. The whole way over, I kept hearing this warning: "Remember, she's really scary. Don't let her intimidate you. She's really, really scary. Don't let her intimidate you." By the time I'd put Norton back in his shoulder bag and we were ringing the woman's front door, I was practically shaking, expecting a cross between The Wicked Witch of the West, Mommie Dearest and the Barbra Streisand who directed *The Prince of Tides* to open up and let us into her lair (in case you're wondering why I identified Babs specifically as the one who directed *The Prince of Tides*, it's because as horrible as I imagine her to be normally, anyone who directed herself in that movie has to be particularly frightening).

I got someone a little different from the way I was picturing her.

When the Nightmare on Wall Street opened her door, she nodded curtly at Zig, basically ignored me totally, went straight over to the cat hanging off my shoulder, stooped down so she was at his eye level, and said something in a high-pitched, babyish voice that was remarkably similar to, "Kitchy kitchy, little kitty, babykins, so happy to see my little baby, oooohhhhh, sweetums . . ."

I thought Ziggy's eyes would pop out of his head because the next thing we both knew, there we were inside this incredibly ritzy beach house and Ziggy's stern, unfeeling, hard as steel client was rolling around on the floor, playing with Norton and cooing at him as if she were a more saccharine version of Shirley Temple.

We wound up staying there over an hour. The only words that were addressed to me were, "I've always wanted to meet him. I'm so honored. Thank you so much." I don't believe that any words were addressed to Ziggy. The rest of the time, we watched in astonishment as she hand fed

Norton, petted him until I think even he was satiated, and told him several hundred times that he was the handsomest devil she'd ever seen.

When the hour was up, she shook my hand, said that Norton was welcome to come back any time he wanted, and then she gave him a giant kiss on the head.

Back in the car, Ziggy couldn't even look at me. We drove in silence until I said, "I can see why she scares you. Does she scratch you under the chin and coo like that at the office?"

"Oh, shut up," he said, which were the last words spoken until he pulled up in our driveway, took Norton's paw in his hand and just said, "Thank you."

To me, he said, "No one I know will believe this."

To Zig—and to Norton—I said, "*Everyone* I know will believe this."

There were other encounters with the rich and famous over the years. Probably the most exciting—and inadvertent—came when Janis and I were taking Norton to the town of Watermill, about ten minutes from Sag Harbor, for another social request.

Our friend Susan Burden had called to say that her parents were visitng from out of town and her mother was a huge Norton fan. Was there any way I could bring him over to meet them, she wanted to know.

Of course there was. I was always happy for Norton to meet and greet his true admirers, so I told Susan that the three of us would be there in half an hour.

We left, as promised, about fifteen minutes after Susan

called, but we had forgotten one little detail. President and Mrs. Clinton happened to be in the Hamptons this particular weekend, fund-raising and hobnobbing and Spielberging and Baldwining. As I made a right turn onto Scuttlehole Road, the street that leads from Sag Harbor to Watermill, we got all of one hundred feet before running into a horde of policemen and barriers and cars with flashing lights. As soon as I saw all this, I realized that I'd read in the local paper that today was the day the president was playing a round of golf at the Atlantic Country Club—which happened to be right on the street to which I'd turned, half a mile farther along. One cop waved us over to the side of the road and indicated that that was as far as we were going for the moment. When I tried to argue that all we wanted to do was go one more measly mile, he shook his head in sympathy but told us it was no go. I then asked how long we'd have to wait and he shrugged in such a way that I knew it meant, "However long it takes to finish eighteen holes, pal."

We waited by the side of the road for about half an hour and then we realized the motorcade was heading our way. We got out of the car—all three of us—and I held Norton up so he could get a view of the history that was passing before our eyes. I also figured there was a slim chance that Socks might be with them—hey, maybe I wasn't the only one who traveled with his cat!—and that this could turn out to be a genuinely inspiring feline moment.

Unfortunately, we never saw Socks. I wouldn't swear that we saw the president or his wife, either, since their limousine zipped by fairly quickly. But I *think* I saw Bill Clinton peering out at us—at a well-dressed woman looking kind of bored, a total slob of a guy in jeans and T-shirt looking impatient, and a small, gray cat being held aloft as he peered at the road trying to see what all the fuss was about. And I think I saw a very familiar expression on the president's face. One I'd seen before.

On Marcello Mastroianni . . .

We had a slightly less auspicious celebrity session one summer. Actually, it was a fairly entertaining experience for me and Norton. It was only disappointing for the others present.

ARF is this valuable and well-run organization in Long Island. The acronym stands for Animal Rescue Fund and they do great work with animals of all kinds. They have a big shelter in Long Island for strays. They have workers who come and play with the animals daily, they have a very moving area which is quarantined off for cats who have leukemia—the sick cats are also played with every day—and they provide tons of good homes for lost, discarded and deserted pets. Every summer, they have some sort of fund-raiser. This year, it was a celebrity tennis tournament. The celebrities playing were Eli Wallach, Charlie Rose, Chuck Scarborough (a longtime New York newscaster), Dina Merrill, George Plimpton, Cliff Robertson and various wealthy and well-known restaurateurs and businesspeople.

Oh yeah. And me.

Now, I do understand that the above list is not exactly the "A" list of celebs these days. But even by these meager standards, I do jump out as a nonfamous person. To ARF, however, I was a god. Not *the* God. But *a* god (Note to the

Christian Right: this is just a semihumorous figure of speech. Please don't send any more outraged letters). I had supported many ARF events in the past, had done several book signings, and, of course, Norton was a revered figure throughout the entire organization. So they decided I was enough of a name to play in their fund-raising matches.

The way it worked was that ten or twelve generous, animal-loving moguls opened up their grand South-hampton estates—particularly their grand tennis courts—and anyone who forked over enough money could play a singles and doubles round-robin tournament with one celebrity. Then all the celebs, ARF workers and donors would meet at one of the estates for lunch and mingling.

The house I was assigned to was magnificent. My house would have fit two or three times over into their en-try hall. Even more demoralizing, it wasn't just their guest house that was bigger and nicer than my place—their *tennis house*, the little shack where they stored balls and rackets—was bigger and nicer than my place. The main house had a pool *and* the guest house had a pool. *And* they had a pri-vate beach right on that little body of water I like to call the Atlantic Ocean. Just for the record, several months after this event, Janis and I saw the very same house listed for sale with Sotheby's—the asking price was sixteen million smackers! I don't know what the guy who owned the house did for a living, but I do know he was around sixty years old and his attractive trophy wife had probably not crossed to the far side of thirty. I also know that when I asked the Missus if I could make a quick phone call, she wanted to know if it was a local call. I thought about offering her a quarter—and muttering as strong an obscenity as I could muster—but instead decided I could wait to call until I got home. I guess if you save a quarter here and a quarter there, pretty soon you've got a sixteen-million-dollar house.

My embarrassing moments weren't over yet. The first one came during the game itself. Janis and Norton were there, of course—ARF had made a special request for my cat's attendance. But no one had told me that there would be actual spectators. As in strangers. But there were. Maybe thirty or forty people were sitting in the bleachers (yes, their tennis court did have bleachers!) doing nothing but watching us play.

I did my best to compose myself. Okay, I decided, so people were watching. No big deal. I was a good tennis player. I was a *very* good tennis player. All I needed was some nerve, right? A little bit of ice water in the old veins. Besides, how good could my first opponent be? Not much better than I was, right? So I thought about Joe Montana driving the Niners 90 yards for a winning touchdown with less than a minute left. I thought about Mariano Rivera coming into a game in the bottom of the ninth with the bases loaded and nobody out and blowing away three straight hitters for the win. I thought about Michael Jordan hitting a shot from the top of the key to win a playoff game with no time on the clock. That's what I *thought* of. Unfortunately, I then proceeded to *play* like Bill Buckner in the tenth inning of Game 6 of the '86 World Series. In my defense, the first guy I played in singles was once a satellite touring pro. Beyond *any* defense was the fact that I couldn't even get my racket on the guy's serve. A normal point went pretty much like this: He'd serve, I'd hear a noise—kind of like a rocket zooming by—and then I'd turn around and see that the ball I was supposed to hit was already behind me. When it was my turn to serve, I'd either hit it straight into the net or I'd hit a beauty right on the baseline and then, whoosh, there was that noise again and somehow the ball would be behind me again. After the first set, he looked like Pete Sampras at Wimbledon. I looked like Jerry Lewis on the dance floor in *You're Never Too Young*.

That wasn't the worst part, however (although it definitely was the worst part for Janis and Norton; Janis told me that after watching the first few games from the bleachers, Norton snuck inside his bag and wouldn't come out again—she said he looked pretty embarrassed that I was his representative). The most humiliating moment came at the luncheon after all the games were done. I overcame my tennis shame to sit with my group as we munched on sandwiches. Norton overcame *his* shame and sat with us. At some point, I realized there was some unhappiness among the munchers and finally I heard one woman say, "And for all this money, we didn't even get a celebrity!" At first I thought maybe I'd just slink away and say nothing. But no. I had to open my mouth. I did a little bit of hemming and hawing and finally worked up the nerve to say, "Um . . . I think *I'm* your celebrity." The woman who had spoken up earlier now spoke up again, with words that will forever ring in my ears. After looking me up and down to make sure there was nothing she was missing, she said, "Well who the *hell* are *you*?!" I did my best to explain about my books and my writing and about Norton—I even tried pushing him into the middle of the group so they could see how irresistible he was—but no one cared. They wanted Leonard Nimoy, not some geeky writer with a humiliated-looking cat.

By this time, I was quite good at reading the expressions on Norton's face, and there was no question that what he was thinking was, *Great. Not only did I have to see some young stud wipe up the tennis court with you, now you make me go through* this!

I was also good at reading the expressions on Janis's face and clearly she was thinking along the same lines. By midafternoon, when we could gracefully make our escape, we were all happy to leave the big-bucks world of Southhampton behind and head back to our smaller-than-a-tennis-shack house.

Not that we were intimidated by celebrities. Not at all. Norton had met his fair share over the course of his life. My favorite combination of all time was Norton and Wilt Chamberlain. I was editing and publishing Wilt's book—and, yes, before you ask, I was the person who asked him how many women he'd slept with and made him put it in the book. Wilt came up to my office a couple of times and, of course, Norton almost always came to the office with me. Seeing a seven-foot-one-and-three-quarter-inch-tall black man sitting on a couch next to a one-foot-tall light gray cat made for a very interesting juxtaposition.

There was another Norton-related sports encounter that also left a deep impression. This one started with a phone call from my GNO pal Andi, who announced that she and her hubby Tom had become friendly with Sandy Koufax. Now, you have to understand that not only am I a baseball loon, but I grew up in Los Angeles in the mid-60's *and* I come from hearty Hebraic stock, so Sandy Koufax ranked up with George Washington, Abraham Lincoln and Martin Luther King as an important historical and cultural figure in my life. When Andi asked if I wanted to come to a small dinner party they were having—to which the greatest living pitcher was also coming—I not only jumped at the opportunity, I immediately called every sports fanatic I knew to tell them all what I was doing. I know a lot of sports writers as well as just plain fans, and each and every one of them warned me about the same thing: Koufax *hated* being fawned over. He did not like talking about himself, he did not like talking about baseball, and he particularly did not like anyone to say these six horrible words: *I'm a big fan of yours.* So for the week leading up to the dinner party, I steeled myself not to fawn. I would picture shaking hands with Koufax, then I'd look in the mirror to make sure that my face betrayed not an iota of idolatry. And most of all I spent hours blanking out the words "I'm a big fan of yours" from my vocabulary.

Well, the night of the dinner party comes and it's a small group, eight in all. Koufax and his girlfriend are the last to arrive. In his absence, I'm still willing myself to look uninterested when I'm introduced. Finally, he enters. Andi, knowing how excited I am to meet him, ushers him over to me. I heard the words, "Peter, this is Sandy Koufax." I give a blasé half turn, barely nod in his direction, hardly even acknowledge his existence, then turn back to whatever conversation I was already having. I wasn't just uninterested, I actually managed to treat him as if he were some dirtball who'd wandered into the wrong house. But I'm feeling pretty good about it, knowing that my mission was accomplished and I didn't embarrass the guy. About a minute passes. Then I feel a slight tap on my shoulder. I turn. It's Sandy. He smiles at me again and says, "I hate doing this but I just have to tell you . . . *I'm a big fan of yours.*"

Yup. Turns out that he had read *The Cat Who Went to*

Paris and had become a Norton nut. He and his ex-wife had even bought a Scottish Fold several years earlier after reading about Norton's adventures. Needless to say, I felt like the world's biggest schmuck. I felt like an even bigger schmuck when, a little later, I found myself telling him about a sore shoulder I had and we were comparing aching arms (in case you don't get where the schmuckdom comes in, my arm was a normal, not very special arm, its most distinguishing characteristic being that it was attached to a hand that could type 80 words a minute; his arm happened to be the greatest single weapon in baseball history and when it finally failed him caused hundreds of thousands of sports fans to weep for untold hours). We did talk about Norton for a good part of the dinner, though, and Sandy—as I call him; well okay, actually I call him Mr. Koufax—was even gracious enough to give me the thrill of a lifetime and talk some baseball with me well into the night.

But our most entertaining encounter with fame came that same summer as the tennis disaster.

It began with a rather odd phone call. It was a hot and perfect Long Island Friday afternoon and I was upstairs in my small office in my small house, pretending to work at my not-so-small computer. What I was really doing was staring out at Janis's backyard garden, trying to figure out how anyone could actually remember the names of different flowers, since the best I've been able to do is come up with "that red one" or "that orange one" or, if I'm really feeling daring, "that kind of reddish orangy one." I was also petting Norton, who was sprawled across the computer keyboard, curled up on his side, looking particularly Muppet-like. He was there partly because he liked being close to me and could always pretty much be counted on to keep me company while I worked, but to be honest, it was mostly because the biggest ray of sunlight was aimed directly on the *d* through *k* keys and he was basking in that warmth. While stroking him, I complimented him on his choice of location. Not only was he able to soak in the sun, he was simultaneously providing me with the perfect excuse not to write.

I lunged at the phone on the first ring (as all writers do when they're pretending to work at their computer) and a woman's voice, with a husky British accent, asked for me by name. In my nonhusky American accent, I told her that it was indeed me she was talking to.

"This is Sybil Christopher," she then said, "and it's *sooo* good to talk to you. Especially because I just discovered, to my horror, that you're not coming to our screening tomorrow night."

A little history now, both to add some local color and so you'll be even more impressed that she was calling me. Sybil Christopher used to be married to Richard Burton (she was the one from whom Elizabeth Taylor stole him during the filming of *Cleopatra*). In the intervening years, she owned and ran a few successful nightclubs, all of them called Arthur, in various chic hot spots around the world, and no doubt did a lot of other interesting things as well. One of the interesting things she was doing now, I knew, was running the small regional theater that had recently opened in Sag Harbor. Because of her contacts and powers of persuasion, the theater had attracted quite a lot of talent, writing as well as acting talent, who wouldn't normally be found exercising their creative muscles on the legitimate stage.

The reason she was calling me, she explained, was because, to raise money for the theater, they were having a special screening, the world premiere of a big new movie. And she'd just found out that I was not on the list of attendees.

I was a little surprised at her horror over this omission, since I'd rarely been invited to anything of this sort, particularly in the Hamptons. On those rare occasions when I *had* been invited, I hadn't gone, since I much prefer staying home and watching sports on TV than going out in public with rich, famous people I don't know. To be perfectly honest, for the most part I'd much prefer being forced to walk over hot coals and having an irate crowd of Fundamentalists poking at my eyes with sticks than going out with rich, famous people I don't know (Okay, cheap gag coming up, but mostly true: the only thing worse is going out with rich, famous people I *do* know). So I began to politely decline her invitation, but she began to—metaphorically—twist my arm. It turns out that she was awfully good at arm twisting, good enough so that pretty soon, much to my surprise, I began to consider showing up. It was a benefit, she told me, and it was totally, *completely* sold out. But she thought she could get *one* more ticket from *somewhere*. Not for free, of course, it *was* a benefit, but it was *only* a hundred dollars a ticket. It was well worth it, I was assured, the movie was wonderful, and *everybody* would be there and it was for *such* a good cause—the theater—and she just felt *so* terrible that she hadn't called earlier . . .

Then she closed the deal very effectively, ending with something I couldn't possibly resist.

"I just can't *believe* you weren't invited," she said. "And neither can *Tony*. He *insists* that you come. He *specifically* asked if you were coming and he'll be *very* disappointed if you're not there."

"He did?" I asked. "And he will?"

"Oh, absolutely," she said. "He'll be *crushed* if you don't come."

"Tony will be *crushed*?"

"No question about it!"

"Oh, well, in that case I guess I'll come," I said, adding, "But you'll have to find two tickets, not one," since I knew that Janis would not be a happy camper if I deserted her on a Saturday night to go off to some fancy movie premiere.

"I'll call you right back," Sybil said, and indeed she did, just a minute or two later, to tell me that, miraculously, she'd found two tickets, that they'd be waiting for me at the box office at the local Sag Harbor movie theater (where the screening was being held) and that I could write a check at my convenience.

I hung up the phone, pondered the fact that I was such a sucker for human contact—if this had been a solicitation by mail, I would definitely have saved myself two hundred bucks and a couple of hours in an old theater that smells like a weird combination of fake butter and liquid cleanser—and went downstairs to tell Janis that we were going to the movies.

When I finished my little explanation, she looked at me, slightly confused, and said, "I didn't know you knew Sybil Christopher."

"I don't," I told her. "Never met her, never spoke to her before."

"And who's *Tony*?" she demanded.

"Absolutely no idea." When she looked even more bewildered, I said, "Clearly, they've made a mistake and they think I'm somebody else. So it'll be fun. Let's go and watch 'em get all confused when whoever they're expecting doesn't show up—and *I do*."

So the next night, a dubious Janis donned her Saturday best—she has an amazing knack for elegance on the spur of the moment—while I put on the ten-year-old ill-fitting sport jacket I keep in Sag Harbor for dress-up emergencies, and we went into town.

First we waited on line to pick up our tickets at the box office. While waiting, I pulled out my checkbook and began writing a check for two hundred smackers. As I was doing so, a rather snotty usher strolled by, saw what I was doing and sniffed, "We don't allow checks."

I could tell he thought this particular check was bouncy enough to play basketball with, and I immediately began to regret my decision to come, but since ushers are, in my mind, on the same intimidating, uniform-wearing authority-figure level as policemen, judges and cable TV repair guys, I started politely explaining how Sybil Christopher said I could write a check and how I only decided to come at the last minute and . . .

"What's your name?" he asked wearily.

"Peter Gethers," I said rather weakly, expecting our evening to end a little earlier than I'd expected.

But weak or not, he practically snapped to attention and said—with a vague tone of reverence, I might add— "Oh, excuse me, Mr. Gethers. You don't even have to wait on line. Just go right inside and tell that usher over there to seat you. And I'm very sorry about the mistake. Of course you can pay by check. Whenever you want."

I raised an eye toward Janis and smiled rather smugly. She shook her head in return. I think she was fairly certain we were on our way to imposter's prison.

The next usher was even more obsequious. "Yes, of course," she practically squealed. "Thank you for coming, Mr. Gethers. You're sitting in the celebrity row, with Tony."

"Good," I said. "I wouldn't want to miss Tony."

Sure enough, she led us to a section right in the middle of the theater with three rows roped off, protected from what I was already beginning to think of as the riff-raff. Sitting in these rows were the usual group of Hamptons celebs: actors, actresses, directors, journalists, owners of media conglomerates, hairdressers, publicists and Dick Cavett (I put Dick Cavett in a separate category because I'm not exactly sure what he is these days; the only thing I do know is that he's at every single gathering of celebrities in the area). The usher lifted the rope and told us which row was ours. We followed instructions perfectly and settled in to watch the rest of the theater start to fill up. Every so often, we'd see a friend or two who'd be off to the side in some crummy seat and who would look surprised to see us smack dab in the middle of Fame Row. When eye contact was made, I'd do something sophisticated and mature like stick my fingers in my ears and wag at them.

Eventually, the place was jammed to the rafters. The only empty seats in the whole theater were the two right next to us. As I was wondering about this fact, I noticed that everyone else was applauding. When I looked around, I realized that the star of the movie and his wife had arrived. Not only that, they were being led to the two empty seats to Janis's right. They sat, nodded cursorily at Janis and waited like everyone else for the lights to dim and the movie to start. This gave us a couple of minutes or so of awkward silence, so Janis leaned over and said to the wife, "Hello, I'm Janis Donnaud."

The wife smiled and said, "I'm Jenny Hopkins. And this is my husband, Tony."

Tony?

As in Anthony?

As in *Anthony Hopkins*? *Sir* Anthony Hopkins? The world's greatest living actor?

Yup.

That's when Janis said, "And this is Peter Gethers."

The sound you're not hearing right now is the longest pause in the world.

Both Mr. and Mrs. Hopkins looked over at me, squinted, stared and said absolutely nothing. And I mean nothing.

"This is where we get sent to the balcony," I whispered to Janis.

But not so fast. Because Anthony Hopkins—Academy Award winner, legend, star of *Silence of the Lambs* and *The Remains of the Day*, which was the movie we were about to watch that night—finally cleared his throat and said to me, in that great, booming Welsh voice of his, "You didn't by any chance bring *Norton*, did you?"

When I tell you that I almost fell off my chair, believe that I'm telling you the truth. At some point, I was able to regain my composure and stutter something along the lines of, "Well, no, actually, I don't usually bring my cat to movie premieres."

And then we started chatting. It turned out that both Hopkins were cat fanatics. Jenny had read *The Cat Who Went to Paris*, fell in love with my little pal, and made Sir Anthony—excuse me, Tony—read it. When Sybil Christopher, an old friend from their days in Wales, invited them to Sag Harbor as a favor to help her theater, they had paced around their flat in London, saying, "Why do we know Sag Harbor? . . . Why do we know Sag Harbor?" Jenny said that, after several days of this, Tony had stopped pacing and suddenly screamed out with eureka-like relief, "That's where Norton lives!" They immediately got on the horn to Sybil, asked if I was coming to the premiere and Sybil, assuming that I must be somebody she should have heard of, got on the horn herself and talked me into forking over the two bills for the tickets.

As the lights in the theater began to dim, Tony leaned across Janis to ask me, "Is there any way we could meet Norton?"

"Sure," I said. And then I realized they were waiting for me to tell them how. "Ummm . . ." I looked at our generation's Olivier and asked, "You wanna come over for breakfast tomorrow?" I immediately began fantasizing about telling my mother how I'd served lox and bagels to Hannibal the Cannibal.

"Oh, we'd love to," Jenny said, "but we have a nine o'clock flight back to London in the morning. We have to leave extremely early."

"You could come for a drink after the movie," I suggested.

"Oh no," Jenny said. "I'm afraid not. There's a little party after the movie and we're sort of the guests of honor."

I was momentarily deflated. Also stumped. Then Tony said, "The party is over at Sybil's theater. Could Norton possibly come to that?"

"I don't see why not," I said. "He's a party animal."

I wasn't at all offended that no one said, "Could *you and Janis* possibly come to that." I was, by this time, quite used to being seen in a subservient role as a companion to my four-legged star. So the minute the movie was over, Janis went over to the theater, accompanied by the Hopkinses, while I drove to my house, pulled out Norton's preferred shoulder bag, and went back to the opening night party—accompanied by my cat.

Now, Norton behaves remarkably well in public situations (often, far better than his dad). But he hadn't actually been to any movie premiere parties. When he's in public, Norton is usually assured of being the biggest celebrity in the joint. That was clearly not going to be the case in this instance. So despite my confident reply to the Hopkinses, I admit to having had a few doubts about the wisdom of this little jaunt.

Once again, I was forced to issue my cat a sincere apology.

Because, of course, he was perfect.

I didn't think that putting him down and letting him wander through the crowd was a great idea (he would have been fine, no question about it, but being a foot tall and walking around on four legs isn't really the ideal situation to be in at a cocktail party; also, I wasn't sure if the bartender knew how to mix a catnip martini and I thought it best to avoid that embarrassing situation). Nor did I think that setting him down on the bar was the best solution (I knew this crowd; standing between them and the alcohol was not a great location if one desired any peace and quiet). Finally, I decided to let him sit in the front row of the theater. I pulled the first aisle seat down, set his bag there and then watched as Norton settled in on top of it and did indeed become the star of the evening. Basically, he sat there calmly, as if attending a play. Or, more accurately, as if he were a member of a royal family receiving visitors. Occasionally, he'd swivel his head to check out his surroundings or if he thought someone was speaking too loudly. The Hopkinses would not leave his side. Jenny, in particular, spent most of the night petting him and telling him what a good boy he was. Gradually, the entire party moved down toward the stage area because that's where Tony and Jenny were—and they were there because that's where Norton was. One by one, everyone came over to congratulate Tony on another brilliant performance and then, one by one, everyone would get asked, "Have you met Norton?" (And yes, you're absolutely right, absolutely no one got asked, "Have you met Peter?")

After a few minutes, I actually relaxed and realized my cat didn't need me hovering around him, so Janis and I drank, ate and mingled with the couple of hundred people who were there to support Sag Harbor's newest cultural attraction. Every so often, I'd make my way back toward the front, check on my Fold who, as near as I could tell, was in heaven in the midst of all this fuss being made over him. At some point, I felt someone tap me on the shoulder, and when I turned around I saw that it was Lauren Bacall.

"Excuse me," she said, smiling graciously. "May I ask you a question?"

With images from *The Big Sleep* and *To Have and Have Not* flashing in front of me, I did my best to look debonair and said, "Of course."

"Well, then, my question's this." Her smile broadened even more graciously as she put her hand on my shoulder and spoke warmly. "I don't know who you are and I don't know why you're here. But if I want to talk to Tony Hopkins, who's an old and dear, dear friend . . . *why do I have to stand in line behind your fucking cat?!*"

I looked toward the front of the theater. There were fifty people or so trying to get in close enough to talk to the Hopkinses. Jenny was holding Norton in her arms and Tony's back was to the crowd while he petted and scratched him. I knew it was impossible in the midst of the din, but I was almost certain I could hear Norton purring above the chatter of the crowd. I turned back to Lauren Bacall.

"It's a long story," I told her. "Believe me. It's a long story."

CHAPTER 7

THE CAT
WHO TURNED
MIDDLE-AGED

t turned out that my cat and I had one more parallel going on in our already entwined lives.

We were both getting a little older.

And feeling it.

My brush with the aches and pains that come with no longer being able to describe oneself by the word "thirty" followed by any known number began with what I can only describe as an excruciating, whimper-inducing pain in my right shoulder. Perhaps you've picked up on the fact that stoicism is not one of the words that leaps to mind when most people try to describe me. Nonetheless, my shoulder hurt like hell and the pain led to various doctor visits, x-rays, MRIs, and ultimately an operation that revealed, among other messy but less serious stuff, degenerative arthritis. The operation was followed by a whole bunch of physical therapy (I was usually in a room with a lot of people who'd had their legs crushed by trucks or their arms ripped out of their sockets by machines I would never actually touch much less operate manually, so I had the double dissatisfaction of being in extreme pain but being way too embarrassed to complain about it). It was also followed by more doctor visits, a discussion of my future prospects with one of those doctors that included the unappealing phrase, "How's your pain tolerance?" and another conversation that ended with this upbeat assessment: "Well, the idea is to keep you as pain free as possible for another fifteen years, then we'll do a shoulder replacement so you can feed yourself and brush your own teeth." I'm leaving out the session where my surgeon explained to me that my body was like a tire that was good for 100,000 miles. When he got to the part pointing out that I'd used up about 50,000 of those miles, I just started making pathetic little noises and begging him to come up with some other analogy. After he told me about the difficulties I was going to have brushing my own teeth I decided that the whole tire thing was fine and told him to stick with that from now on.

All in all, although Janis might disagree if I let her insert her own paragraph at this point, I think I handled the pain and trauma (and acceptance that gradually I was disintegrating and falling apart and would soon be little more than a pile of rotting garbage in this stinking, crummy world) with great maturity and grace. I might even go so far as to use the words "regal nobility." However, when my cat got sick and began showing similar signs of middle-age wear and tear, I totally fell apart.

Janis, Norton and I had made another Christmastime trip to Sicily to visit the Tornabenes in their fourteenth-century abbey, and when we returned, I noticed something strange. The water in Norton's water bowl was disappearing very quickly.

I didn't really think anything of it, other than, after a couple of weeks of this, it occurred to me that my cat didn't usually drink a lot of water. At first I thought that maybe my apartment and my house in Sag Harbor were both overheated and that the water was evaporating. I know, this sounds crazy (as well as pretty dumb) but it just never occurred to me that Norton would be lapping up an entire bowl or two of water a day. Then, the next thing I realized was that not only was the water in his bowl disappearing but Norton was suddenly drinking water out of the toilet. At all hours of the day and night, I'd hear that unmistakable sound of animal tongue taking in water as quickly as possible, head in to the bathroom and find Norton leaning into the bowl and drinking like a . . . well . . . like a commonplace *dog*. For a day or two, I did nothing but mull this over and think it was odd. Now you have to understand that for our entire mutual existence, I treated my cat exactly as I would treat myself (except for those occasions when I treated him better). By that, I mean that I believed in living well and making life as easy as possible for myself—and by extension, I wanted him to live as well as I did and have as easy a life. One of the things I didn't do for myself was to go to the doctor very often. I'm not a hypochondriac and I'm not a very fearful person. I also tend toward fatalism and generally think that things will run their proper course. On the other hand, I'm not a total cretin and I'm not above seeking help when help is needed. So after a few days of puzzling over Norton's behavior, just as I would have done over mine if I'd suddenly started lapping up water out of the toilet bowl, I decided that something had to be wrong and that it was time to take him to the vet.

Since kittenhood, Norton had been a lucky guy. Not only was he rarely ill, he had an absolutely sensational vet in Sag Harbor named Dr. Jonathan Turetsky. Jonathan is not only a caring and loving doctor, he is stunningly thorough. Whenever I'd take Norton in for his annual checkups, I'd come home to Janis and say that I wished *my* doctor was as thorough in his probing and analysis. I loved Turetsky. As did almost all his patients—both paying bipeds and sick quadrupeds.

Unfortunately Norton couldn't stand him.

It drove the good doc crazy. For years, he'd greet Norton warmly, talk to him soothingly, treat him wonderfully, genuinely care about his welfare—and my friendly, charming, perfect cat would act as if he were being examined by one of the flying monkeys in *The Wizard of Oz*. All Turetsky had to do was get near him and Norton would hiss and scratch and do his best impersonation of Charles Bronson in *The Great Escape* trying to get out of the tunnel.

As everyone knows by now, Norton went everywhere, all over the world, not just uncomplainingly but willingly. Put him in a car, he'd be happy. Sitting in my lap on a plane, no problem, only pleasure. Trains, boats, you name it (other than the basket on the front of a bicycle, an unpleasant experiment which is best left unspoken) and Norton was happy and compliant. There was only one consistent exception: if I put him in the car to head over to see his vet. When that happened, the second he'd hit the seat he'd start howling like a banshee. We're talking wolflike baying at the

moon. I have no idea how he always knew we were heading down Route 114 to Turetsky's office on Goodfriend
Drive—especially since we often drove that route without
going to the doctor—but he always did and he always cried
every inch of the way. To make matters worse for Turetsky's feelings of self-worth, after several years of treating
Norton, he brought a new doctor in to the practice, with
the great name of Dr. Pepper. It doesn't sound so bad if you
throw in his first name, Andrew, but there's no way I can
resist just calling him Dr. Pepper. Well, Norton was absolutely fine with Pepper. No hysteria, no cowering in the
corner, no pleading looks at me to fork over his transit papers and get him out of Casablanca. This caused even more
head shaking for Doc Turetsky but he seemed to accept this
strange response and when it came time for him to do
things medicinal that Norton particularly hated—like taking blood; that was Norton's least favorite thing in the
whole world—he'd often step (and put his ego) aside and
let Dr. Pepper do them. I found it touching that he was so
sensitive to a cat's needs and tried to explain to Norton that
he was lucky to have such a touchy-pawy guy at his beck
and meow. But it was no go. No matter how sensitive the
treatment, Turetsky was still the Nazi and Pepper was the
allied soldier coming to the rescue.

Which made it all the more strange when, trying to get
to the bottom of Norton's sudden and insatiable thirst, he
willingly sat on Dr. Turetsky's sterile-looking stainless steel
table in the examining room and let the doc poke and stab
and stick and mutter and squint and weigh and put his gentle hands wherever he wanted. In addition to the fact that
Norton was being so passive, I could tell by the expression

on Turetsky's face that something was wrong. But he wouldn't tell me what. Not until they got the results of the blood test back, he said.

When Norton heard the words "blood test," his out-of-character docileness instantly reverted to his normal anti-Turetsky aggression (okay, that's a slight exaggeration, it wasn't when he heard the words; but when Turetsky took out the needle and tried to take blood, Norton fought back like the jungle beast one of his long ago ancestors actually was). As usual, they had to sedate my poor little cat so they could take some blood and I had to leave him there for an hour or so, until he was over the sedation.

After coming back to get him, the blood test complete, I nervously drove Norton the couple of miles back to the house and waited for twenty-four hours until we'd get word.

During that twenty-four-hour period I, of course, feared the worst. Although I didn't have any idea what the worst was. I did know that Norton had lost two pounds, which for a nine-pound cat, is quite a lot. I was kicking myself for not noticing how skinny he'd gotten, guilty that my ignorance had led him to whatever horrible thing it was I was sure he had. I was pacing and nervous and, every few minutes, picking Norton up into my arms, cradling him and kissing him and telling him that everything was going to be fine. Janis kept assuring me that everything actually *would* be fine, but my usually optimistic nature suddenly deserted me. When the doctor called me the next day in the early afternoon and told me to come back, with cat in tow, I was a wreck. I didn't ask Janis to come with us, but she didn't have to be asked. She knew this was unlikely to be my shining hour, so she just headed out with me when I put Norton on my shoulder, and came along to lend support.

By the time we got to Dr. Turetsky's animal clinic—with Norton yowling the entire way, as usual—I was even more of a wreck. Since I'd decided he was now riddled with disease, he looked like a totally different cat to me. Suddenly, I was thinking he'd lost half his body weight and was totally skeleton-like. I was convinced the meow I was listening to wasn't just the usual I-hate-the-vet complaint but had to be filled with pain. I also thought his glare was a bit disdainful since I'd clearly ignored the dire symptoms for a few weeks and let him dehydrate. By the time we stepped into Turetsky's examination room, I was drenched in sweat and felt as if I'd aged ten years.

I put Norton down on the steel table, watched him sneak a suspicious glance at his old enemy, then listened as Dr. Turetsky said, calm as could be, "Don't get too upset when I tell you what I'm about to tell you, because we've caught it very early and it's not a tragedy, but Norton's got the beginning of kidney failure."

I took a deep breath. Then another. I tried to stay calm. I thought, *Well, fine, now I've heard the news and I can deal with it. I'm a mature human being and I can definitely deal with it.*

Who was I kidding? Here's exactly what went through my mind when I got the diagnosis:

Kidney *failure*. Not kidney *disease*. Failure = hopeless. Hopeless = dead. Oh, my God, my cat's dying!

I kept a stoic face but I was sure this was it. I was just as sure that the doc had no idea how shaken I was until I heard the words, "Norton's going to be fine, but I think you'd better sit down so you don't pass out."

Much to my chagrin, I took a seat as Janis reached for my hand to give it a reassuring squeeze. My heart was racing and I realized I was trembling. Norton was still seated on the shiny stainless steel, looking not at all perturbed.

"How long does he have?" I asked, expecting to hear the words, "Two or three days," but Turetsky said, "He's not dying. Honest. This is very common in older cats and it can be contained for quite a while. If it doesn't get any worse, he can live for many years."

I managed to say, "Contained? Does that mean 'cured'?"

"No," Turetsky explained. "Kidney failure is irreversible. We can't fix it but what we can do is try to make sure it doesn't get any worse. We've caught it extremely early, the tests show that certain elements in his blood are higher than normal but there's nothing that's remotely approaching a crisis. And Norton is extremely healthy otherwise. I've seen cats live for four or five years, even longer, with this kind of thing."

Because Turetsky obviously thought he was giving me good news, he immediately went on to explain all sorts of things to me: what the levels of Norton's blood test meant, the type of treatment he'd need, what I should look for in his behavior, and I'm sure all sorts of other things, but I wasn't actually hearing one word. I was staring off into space, trying really hard to keep tears from welling up in my eyes, with my thoughts jumbled and sad and terrible.

I remember thinking, *Four or five years, well, that's a long time, that's fine, he's already thirteen . . .*

And I also remember thinking, *Four or five years?! No, no, that's impossible, that's not long enough, I want him for many, many years more than that . . .*

And then I remember thinking, *I can't believe it. My cat's not going to live forever . . .*

At some point, I'm going to be without Norton . . .

While the concerned vet rambled on, I did my best to nod and look like I had some idea what he was saying. I did hear a few phrases such as, "I know you're very attached to your cat," and, "We all know how special Norton is so we're going to do everything we can," but basically I didn't have a clue what was going on.

Turetsky clearly knew I was shaken because at some point he said, "I think with the proper treatment, Norton's going to be fine. But if it ever comes to that, there's even a new operation that involves kidney transplants for cats."

This perked me up. I knew people who'd had kidney transplants who lived twenty, thirty years, even longer.

"I'd definitely be willing to do that," I said.

Turetsky started to say that it wasn't necessary, that it was way too early to even consider, but Janis interrupted him. "No," she explained to him, "he doesn't mean he'd be willing to let Norton have the operation, he's saying he'd give Norton his kidney."

The doctor nodded appreciatively (although I'm sure he was secretly storing this one away to share over several martinis at the next vet convention) then explained, without coming close to laughing, that it was a very nice offer and it was rare to see that kind of bond between man and cat, but the truth was that my kidney would be a bit *large* for Norton. The way it worked, he said—and I have to admit, even in my sudden state of grief, I thought this was extremely cool—was that when they did a kidney transplant on a cat, they took a healthy but homeless cat, removed one kidney, and gave it to the sick cat. The only stipulation is that the owner of the sick cat then had to adopt the donor cat and give it a good home. I thought this was more than fair and he told me that if it ever reached that stage, most of the transplant research was being done in California and he'd get me more information. Then he looked at Janis, smiling slightly, and said, "How did you know that's what he meant? About the kidney."

"Because I know him," she said. "You have to understand, he'd give up all of his limbs for this cat."

"Yes," he told her. "I've been treating both of them long enough so I think I do know that. And not only that, I think I understand it."

One of the reasons I liked Turetsky so much is that I think he even approved.

So now that we were over the first hurdle and I realized I could keep all my own organs, he started explaining exactly what I was going to have to do.

The first thing he did was show me a foot-long plastic bag filled with a clear liquid. I remember him saying something about Norton needing an injection once a week or once every two weeks, depending on his progress. The purpose was to keep him hydrated and to keep his kidney from becoming overworked. And I definitely remember him saying something along the lines of, "I'll show you how easy it is." Then, while Norton was still sitting on the table, Turetsky hung the bag up on a hook several feet above the cat, connected some sort of tube to the bottom, and picked up a box which I could see was filled with needles. He lifted off a small plastic covering from one of the needles to reveal its sharp edge. Then he inserted the needle into the end of the tube—and stuck it into my little cat.

"It's not like a hypodermic," he said. "You don't have

to find a vein. It's strictly a subcutaneous drip. It just has to break the skin and it can go in anywhere. Then you leave it in until he gets a hundred milliliters of liquid."

My eyes widened as I could see the clear liquid flowing into Norton, gathering in his body toward his back legs. When Turetsky decided he'd had enough, he pulled the needle out and I stared at Norton, who was clearly unfazed but looked like he'd swallowed an orange—whole. He had a big round bulge that was sloshing around under the skin.

"That's the liquid," Turetsky said, touching the squishy bulge. "It's just a saline solution. And it'll take a few hours for it to absorb into his blood system." Then he looked at me, saw that my eyes were bulging almost as far as the mound in Norton's midsection, and asked, "Are you all right?"

"I think so," I said. "Except I do have one question."

"Anything," he said.

"Are you saying I'm supposed to stick that needle in my cat and do what you just did?"

"Yup," Dr. Turetsky said.

And that's when I knew that my life was about to change.

Drastically.

I was a bit more relaxed when I left Dr. Turetsky's office. For one thing, although I was still traumatized at the thought of my cat's frailty and lack of immortality, I pretty much accepted the fact that I was in no immediate danger of having him scamper on up to the Great Kennel in the

Sky. For another thing, Turetsky assured me that if I couldn't/wouldn't/didn't want to be the one to stick the needle into Norton's flesh, someone there would do it for me—for a fee, of course. And that's what I did for the next few weeks. I must admit that I used my bad shoulder as an excuse right off the bat, saying that I couldn't rig the drip-thing up, hold on to Norton and keep the needle in place all at the same time because I didn't have the mobility. But the truth was that it was inconceivable to me that I could stick a sharp object into my beloved cat's body and fill him full of saline solution. I just couldn't do it. I was certain I'd hurt him, which was the worst thing I could imagine in life. And—I hate confessing this to all you cat lunatics who might actually have some respect for me—I was way, way, *way* too squeamish.

There. I admit it. I was a major league wimp.

I remember telling my parents, back in those oh-so-great days of the '60s that they'd never have to worry about me becoming a drug addict because the mere idea of sticking a needle into my own arm—or worse, letting some drugged-out, Hot Tuna–loving hippie named Free stick a needle into my arm—was enough to make me vote for Richard Nixon (okay, that's a slight exaggeration, but not *much* of one). I always figured if I got diabetes and had to inject myself with insulin, that'd be it for me. Couldn't do it. Uh-uh. No how, no way.

Worse, it wasn't just my aversion to needles. I knew I simply wasn't a natural caregiver. I didn't know if I was ca-pable of it. I was uncomfortable around disease, even more uncomfortable around someone else's pain. My logic al-ways was, that's why I make money, so I can afford to let somebody else deal with that stuff. The closest I'd come to experiencing all of that was when my father had cancer. But even then, while I certainly went through the emotional agony that comes with a father's decline and death, I was three thousand miles away for the worst of it and wasn't really present until the dirty stuff was over with—and only the sad stuff remained.

Sad, I could deal with.

The rest of it . . . well . . . I really didn't think so.

Nonetheless, when it came to Norton, I tried. I really did. But this against-my-nature effort was one of the great fiascos of my life, cat-related or anything-else-related.

We were in the city and I was thinking about the drip bag and the whole IV thing and I decided I could do it. I decided I *had* to do it. Turetsky had shown me how and so had one of the women who worked in his clinic. They made it look easy. Norton didn't seem to mind being stuck. And they even gave me a valuable tip: they said that sometimes the liquid was too cold and it shocked the cat when it hit his system, so they told me to put the bag in a sink with hot water for a few minutes to warm it up and make the process more palatable.

So once I made the decision that it was full steam—or saline solution—ahead, that's what I did first. I ran hot water in my bathroom sink, put the bag in for five minutes, then pulled it out. I touched the outside of the plastic and it felt too hot to me. I took a difficult breath and grappled with the following worry: what if I scald the inside of my cat?

I almost gave it up then and there but decided no, I was doing this. So I let the bag lie out of the water for a couple of minutes, then touched it again. Now it felt too cold. I put it back under the hot water, standing there, touching it every fifteen seconds or so, until it felt close to a comfortable temperature. Then I dried it off in a towel and realized that I hadn't even started yet and I was already ready for a nap.

Try to picture this now. I go to my dining room table which, for some unknown reason, struck me as the right place to attempt this procedure. I laid Norton's shoulder bag on the table, because I knew he found the bag comforting, and then I put Norton on top of the bag. He seemed curious but not adverse to staying there. In fact, he relaxed, stretched his back feet out behind him and his front paws out in front of him, which was his distinct, Sphinx-like and very odd way of getting comfortable. So far so good. Although I have to admit, I was not just exhausted from the whole procedure already, I was already sweating.

Next: I've got this foot-long plastic bag filled with liquid. With slightly warm liquid. I know I've got to hang it up on something, so it can function as an IV and the liquid will drip down into my cat. I've got a chandelier above my dining table—ah ha! That must have been the reason I thought this was a good location—so I hook the bag up to the chandelier. Step Two is done (Really Step Three, if you count putting Norton on the table, which I definitely do) and, although my hands are now trembling, I'm feeling pretty good. I notice that Janis is watching me from a couch in the living room. I tell her that everything's going great so far. I really feel like I'm on top of it, I say. Supportive as always, she mentions that it's just taken me fifteen minutes to put the cat on the table and hang up the drip bag. When Turetsky did this procedure, the whole *thing* took *five* minutes.

Ignoring her dig, I decided I was ready for the tough stuff.

First was a little mechanical maneuver. I had to attach a plastic tube to the drip bag. This couldn't be simpler. All that's involved is pulling a small tab off a little white piece of plastic that's on the bottom of the bag, then punch some weird pointed thing that's at one end of the tube right through it. Easy. Except I'm not the most mechanical person in the world. I remember being in high school once and taking one of those tests to show you what kinds of skills you have that might be useful in later life. I thought the test was fairly easy for the first half hour or so, then I got to the part that tested you on spatial relations and mechanical ability. I got to one diagram that showed two gears touching each other. The question below it said, "If gear *A* spins one way, connects to gear *B* at this point, which way will gear *B* spin?" I spent the rest of the allotted two hours staring blankly and hopelessly at the two gears, realizing that if they left me in the room for a million years I would not be able to answer the question. So even though this little plastic doohickey on the drip bag seemed idiot-proof, I hesitated. When I was sure I had the right end of the tube and the right piece of plastic, I did my thing.

It worked!

The tube was in. All systems were go. Houston, we have *no* problem!

Except now Norton wasn't on the table. He was over on the couch sitting next to Janis, watching me much the same way she was. Which was dubiously.

I sauntered over, very confident now, picked him up and put him back on the table.

And he hopped right off again.

We went through this routine about ten times until finally I got him to stay. I kept saying to Janis, "See? This is a good sign. He's feeling so good he doesn't even *want* his drip. And look at the way he's running around. This is very, very good." And she kept saying back to me, "Okay, it's good. But it would be even better if you could do this sometime in the next twenty-four hours so we can get on with our lives."

Now I was ready. Norton was on the table, relaxed, if still looking a bit dubious. The bag was all hooked up (it did occur to me that the liquid had probably cooled down by now, but I decided Norton and I could both live with that for this first time), and all that was needed was the needle.

I had a Baggie full of needles. I liked this part. It made me feel like I should be hanging out with the guys from Stone Temple Pilots. The woman in Turetsky's office had given me some needles that were covered with protective green caps and other needles that were covered with pink caps. The green needles were big, the pink ones were little. They told me to try the pink first, they would be easier. It would take longer for the liquid to drip, but the insertion process would be simpler. So I rummaged in the Baggie and pulled out a pink capped needle. I inserted it into the end of the tube, exactly as Turetsky had shown me, twisted the protective pink cap to remove it and *voilà*! I was all set up. The bag was in place, the needle was exposed and in my hand and ready for insertion. All I had to do was . . . do it. Get the needle in, slide the switch on the tube that started and stopped the flow of liquid, get the needle out, pet the cat, drink an entire bottle of wine as quickly as possible (that last was my own addition to Turetsky's litany of instructions; by that point, I definitely needed it).

I did my best to gather up a little mound of Norton's skin in the fingers of one hand, as they had shown me. With the other hand, I slowly brought the needle closer to him. I realized that I could barely swallow, my throat was so dry. All I could think about was, *What if I hurt him?* My basic premise in dealing with Norton was that I'd rather die than hurt him. But they told me it *wouldn't* hurt. It sure didn't seem to hurt when Turetsky did it. In fact, Norton looked kind of bored with the entire process. So if Turetsky could do it, so could I. Right?

Sure.

I stuck my cat with the needle, knowing everything would now go smoothly. Except the second I touched him, he flinched.

The second he flinched, I drew back, terrified that I'd done something bad. And the second I drew back, he leapt off the table.

There I was holding the needle, with no cat, and somehow the liquid in the drip bag was now spurting out all over my dining table. I looked like a fireman putting out a blaze more than I looked like a concerned pet owner trying to perform the simplest maneuver possible on an under-the-weather cat.

I flicked the little switch on the tube—which somehow I had touched when I flinched—and managed to stop the gushing liquid. Then I got up from the table and went and got my cat. Again, I put him on the table and again he lay down—although he was definitely not as relaxed as he'd been. Of course, neither was I. In fact, my heart was pounding so hard, I was reasonably sure I was in the midst of a heart attack. I could hear Janis do her best not to snicker, and I decided, okay, this is it, I'm definitely doing this . . .

The needle went in.

Then out.

And the next thing I knew, there was blood everywhere. I tried repeatedly to get the thing into my cat, absolutely couldn't do it, and by the time he jumped off the table and scampered into a closet, I was fairly sure I'd killed him because I had never *seen* so much blood.

"Get the cat!" I started screaming at Janis. "I think I hurt him really bad!"

I couldn't understand why she was laughing.

"I'm not kidding!" I yelled. "I think I stabbed my cat to death!"

"I don't think you touched your cat," Janis said calmly. Well, not so calmly. It's hard to be calm when you're laughing that hard.

"*What* are you laughing at?" I asked, infuriated that she wasn't taking me seriously. And even angrier that she didn't seem to care that I was going to be imprisoned for cruelty to the feline species. And then I realized what was amusing to her. She was right—I hadn't even come close to getting the needle into my cat's skin. What I'd done with that razor sharp little fucker was stab myself—in my fingers, in my arm, in my thigh, in almost every part of my body—about 140 times. Every time I moved, I managed to stick it into some other place where skin was exposed. The blood was all mine.

I gave a huge sigh of relief now that I knew I'd done no harm to my trusting Fold. The relief didn't last too long, though. It disappeared when I realized I might actually pass out at the sight of all my blood.

"I think it's back to Turetsky," Janis said.

"Yeah," I agreed. "But first call an ambulance, okay?"

That was enough to convince me that I was not cut out for this. So for the next three weeks in a row, Janis, Norton and I headed out to Sag Harbor for the weekend and on Friday or Saturday, I'd take Norton in to Turetsky's office, one of the aides would fill him up with fluid, I'd fork over twenty bucks, and then we'd go on our merry way. With all my blood *inside* my body, where it belonged.

For those three weeks, life was good. Then my relaxed state ended because I was suddenly convinced that Norton was on his last legs after all.

This relapse turned out to be another false alarm, but I didn't accept this until I had my first up close and personal experience with Dr. Marty Goldstein.

I had, not long before Norton's kidney diagnosis, come in contact with Dr. Marty (as he's often called by the pet owners who swear by him) in my professional capacity. An agent had called me, said she'd discovered the most amazing vet in the world, a *holistic* vet, and she thought there was a big book in it. I agreed to drive with the agent up to Marty's veterinary office in South Salem, about an hour and a half away in upstate New York, to see what all the fuss was.

The fuss was, in fact, fairly amazing.

The first thing one notices about Marty Goldstein is that he's your basic goofball. He wears ties with stupid-looking dogs on them and has weird cartoons of animals all over his office and I'm pretty sure that at our first meeting he was wearing one of those hats with big, floppy dog ears on it hanging down from each side. He has *Far Side* cartoons on his walls, he cracks wise constantly, is generally pretty silly, and he's more reminiscent of Pee Wee Herman than, say, George Clooney in "ER."

And then one notices something else about Dr. Marty: he's a little bit of a miracle worker.

I can't remember being so jazzed as I was by the end of our first meeting. We got a little lecture which explained the meaning of and philosophy behind holistic and naturopathic animal healing, then we were treated to a series of illustrated case studies. In many of these cases, animals— mostly cats and dogs with some form of cancer—were brought to Marty by owners who reported that other vets had said it was time for euthanasia. In an astounding number of instances, Marty didn't just prolong the lives of these animals, he cured them. We looked at photo after photo of disease-ridden pets who looked to be on death's door, and then saw follow-up photos, some of them taken years later, of these same animals looking happy and, more important, healthy.

Over dinner that night, Marty further expounded on his beliefs and why he thought they were not just right but genuinely important. He explained that veterinary medicine, much like the medical system for humans, was dominated by greed, which often led to easy and false diagnoses. He talked about how important diet was for animal health—same as it was for humans—and how misguided conventional medicinal treatments often were because they were geared toward stifling the symptoms of disease rather than dealing with the disease itself. He also talked about how crucial it was to maintain an animal's health when he was in a state of remission rather than to simply treat and try to cure an animal when he was already ill. It made an awful lot of sense. And what I liked best about Marty is that he wasn't a total New-Age nut. Sure, he was a proselytizer, because he believed passionately in his cause. But he was also someone who had graduated from the Cornell University College of Veterinary Medicine and who had once been a conservative, by-the-book vet. When he began his practice, he said he used 5 percent holistic treatments and 95 percent standard Western veterinary treatments. Over the next fifteen years or so, as he saw standard treatments fail to address the needs of his patients, that ratio had become reversed. Nonetheless, there were cases where he still definitely urged the use of antibiotics and other conventional medicines, and he certainly believed in operations when they were necessary.

I came away convinced—and signed Marty up to write a book for Alfred A. Knopf, one of the country's most prestigious publishing houses and one of the houses for which I work.

Of course, like many people, I was theoretically convinced—but I didn't apply my convictions to my own life.

Until, that is, a month or so after Norton's first injection in Dr. Turetsky's office, when he became very, very lethargic. One day, I noticed he seemed sluggish. Then, for the next two or three days, he didn't eat and he hardly moved. I did what I always did in such situations with my cat—I panicked. I took him to Turetsky, who, after finding out Norton had lost yet another pound—he'd now lost about a third of his total body weight—put him on antibiotics. Another week passed and Norton didn't seem any better. I was worrying more than ever. Even I could see that he was looking bad. And he hardly ever left his spot on the floor. He was beginning to resemble a furry rug more than an actual living, breathing cat.

It was Janis, naturally, who told me to call Marty Goldstein.

"You thought he made so much sense," she said, "why don't you see what he has to say?"

So I called Marty, told him about Norton's diagnosis and his current lethargy and loss of weight, and waited for him to say, "Sorry, there's nothing I can do, your cat's got about an hour to live." Instead, here's what he said: "Oh, sure, no problem. I can fix this in a day."

"You can?" I said, stupefied.

"Don't worry about it. Call your vet and ask him to fax me a copy of the blood test. Then I'll overnight you a few supplements and herbs for Norton. Follow the instructions, they're not complicated, and he'll be fine."

"That's it?" I asked. "And he will?"

"After you give him the stuff, call me the next day and let me know what you think."

So I called over to Turetsky's office, asked them to fax the test, which they did, and the next day I received a package containing four or five different supplements and herbs, which I was to give Norton by dropper.

I was quite skeptical but did as I was told. The bottles all had words like "renal" and "hepaticol" and "glandular" printed on them, words which at the time meant nothing to me, but I followed orders and Norton accepted his medicine as docilely as he'd accepted everything else the past week.

As Janis is my witness—and she is—I woke up the next morning to find Norton meowing his head off, waiting in the kitchen to be fed. I started to feed him, as usual, then suddenly stopped myself. I looked over at my cat with wonder. He was not only waiting to be fed, he was clearly ravenous. And he not only gobbled down every last bit of food, when he was done he began running around the living room of the Sag Harbor house as if he were a kitten.

A *little* kitten.

A little, *healthy* kitten.

I have to say, I ran up the stairs, shook Janis awake and said that Norton was not only moving, he was moving in a way he hadn't moved in years. She started to go downstairs to check it out for herself but she didn't have to, because you-know-who had already bounded upstairs and had jumped on the bed, looking pretty damn happy about it, too. I immediately went to the phone and called Dr. Marty.

"I guess you know what you're doing," I told him.

"We still have more work to do," he said. "Make an appointment and bring Norton in to see me."

I responded with the only thing I felt to be appropriate under the circumstances: "Yes, sir," I said. "Whatever you want."

I took Norton up to South Salem to see the holistic vet a few days later.

We went into Marty's examining room and he came in wearing his usual nutjob outfit (I think this one included a vest with dumb-looking jungle animals all over it). Norton was, by this time, his usual self—confident, unafraid and curious. In fact, while we were waiting for Marty to join us in the room, my cat was climbing all over everything, checking the place out. When Marty came in, he picked

Norton up and cradled him, talking to him like they were old pals. He went on like that for a few minutes—I could see that Norton had taken an instant shine to him and was relaxed—and then Marty set the cat down and spoke to me. And what he spoke about was kidney failure. His words didn't make me nervous or depressed. He dealt with the disease as if it were an absolutely natural and normal part of life—which, of course, it is—and he spoke about it as if there was nothing to fear. He assured me that Norton was indeed in the beginning stage of kidney failure, but he also said that other than that, he was healthy. And then he did something wonderful: he explained to me the various stages of what Norton would go through if the disease went on to its natural end. He said that—and he stressed that this was way, way in the future—eventually what would happen is that when the kidney went into serious failure, Norton would get logy and then even logier, he would lose much of his energy and would start napping more. Eventually, he would fade away into this drowsy state, go into a coma and die. Marty looked at me and said, "When the time comes, it's absolutely painless and easy. Believe me, if you could choose a way to die, it would be kidney failure." He took a breath, then said, "Anyway . . . I just want you to know what it is we've got here. I think the more you know, the better off you are. And the less fear you'll have."

Even though he was dealing with the subject of death—granted, not mine, but still, the next closest thing as far as I was concerned—his words made me feel better. More relaxed and more accepting of what I would eventually be forced to accept. It reminded me a lot of when my father died. He wanted to die at home—he had cancer—

and we were more than happy to oblige. The last few days of his life he was set up in a hospital bed in his bedroom and we had a wonderful nurse from a hospice who stayed with him most of the time. A few days before his death, she spoke to me, my brother and my mother and told us what was going to happen. She described the process we would witness—the process of dying—and she explained exactly what was going to happen physically. She told us that, when the time came, we would see him relax, actually see a certain pleasure on his face and in his eyes. She said that's what people meant when they talked about a glow or a light that seemed to surround dying people. She urged us to touch him, both when he was alive and after he died, so we would know that death was nothing to fear. It was quite a comforting speech, mostly because it rang true. When that time did finally come, I wasn't there to witness it. Janis and I were out buying groceries and when we pulled the car into the garage, my brother and my mom both came out to say that my dad was dead.

To be truthful, there was a part of me that was secretly glad I had missed the final moment. I felt bad that I wasn't with my family but there was no denying that death also frightened me. I didn't really want to be quite so close to it and there was a large part of me that felt that by not confronting it head on, I didn't fully have to accept its existence. Oh, I knew it existed, it's not like I was in a total state of denial. I just didn't particularly feel like touching it.

So, my new veterinary advisor made me feel better and I thought his words rang true. But now it was time for action and I wanted to see what he was going to do for Norton.

Marty told me that he wanted to run his own blood test

on Norton. He asked the lab for different and deeper analyses on certain things, he said. I told him that was fine, but that Norton would absolutely refuse to let his blood be taken unless he was sedated. I hurriedly explained that my cat was perfect—except in this one instance. Marty told me that he wouldn't have a problem and I said, "No, really, I know my cat extremely well. He's the most gentle animal on earth, honest, but he's never, ever, *ever* let a vet take his blood without things looking a lot like the fourteenth round of Ali-Frazier III."

Marty nodded, totally dismissing my warning, and picked Norton back up into his arms. He spoke very gently to the cat. Not in cat language or anything, don't worry, this isn't one of those "ma" and "fa" moments from *Day of the Dolphin*, but he stroked him gently, whispered to him, and within a few seconds he told the nurse, who had suddenly appeared, to prepare the hypodermic. I shook my head, expecting the worst. Marty took the syringe, whispered something else to Norton, looked him straight in the eye and jabbed the needle in. Norton didn't even blink. Not so much as a whimper or an attempted scratch. He just looked right back at Marty, gave him that okay-I-trust-you look, and let the guy take his blood.

I couldn't believe it. It crossed my mind that maybe it was one of those fake syringes, the kind you buy for Halloween, and that I was dealing with a total loon, but then I saw the blood rise up into the small vial and I knew I was on to something special here (this scene was repeated, about a year later, with my friend Paul. Marty didn't take Paul's blood, but he did take the blood of Paul's idiot golden retriever dog, Buddy. Buddy, a neurotic mess of a canine who has a nasty habit of barking at rocks all day long, made

Norton's blood-taking phobia look mild. When Marty went forward with the needle, Paul warned him that there was a fifty-fifty chance that Buddy would actually bite his fool head off. Marty just waved him away, looked Buddy right in the eye and did what he had to do. According to Paul, when it was all over, Buddy was so entranced, he did everything but shine Marty's shoes and tip him twenty bucks).

When Marty had finished examining Norton, he told me that as soon as he got the results, he'd send me a whole bunch of new supplements and herbs, geared for the deficiencies he discovered in the report. He also told me to immediately change Norton's diet, that this was the single most important thing I could do. I said that I would, asked him what he recommended, and he told me. And this is something I've got to do a little proselytizing about on my own now.

I became a big believer in this holistic, naturopathic stuff, came to comprehend the logic behind it, but I understand if people dismiss it as voodoo. I never—and would never—give myself over to it 100 percent. I never did anything for Norton without getting a second, more traditional opinion and then weighing the consequences if the two opinions differed drastically. But the one thing I'm absolutely convinced of is that cats (and dogs, for that matter, there's no need to exclude them from this) deserve better food than what we give them. The way Marty convinced me that I'd been doing my cat wrong all these years was he pulled out a food chart. At the top was what cats eat in their natural habitat—in other words, what their systems naturally go for without human interference. At the bottom was what was actually inside a can of Ken-L Ration and the most common commercial brands. In-between were various other forms of cat food, the so-called health food brands like Science Diet. In their natural habitat, cats ate grains and meat and poultry. Thanks to us humans, what cats mostly eat now are plastic, bone, corn syrup and things I can't even bring myself to mention. Marty's food lecture was a lot like watching the movie *Scream*: I wanted to cover my eyes because it was so scary but I had to see who was going to get slaughtered next.

That afternoon, as soon as I got home, I threw out all my cans of normal cat food and went to a pet health food store to buy cases of the good stuff (in case you're interested, the healthy brands of commercial cat food include Solid Gold, Natural Life, Wysongs, Cornucopia, Preside, PetGuard and Abady; they all use chunks of real meat, whole rather than processed grains, essential vitamins and minerals, and no preservatives). But even as I bought them, I knew I'd only be using them as backups. Because the one thing that Marty convinced me of was that I should be cooking for my cat.

Please. Do me a favor. I'm sure there are some of you who are nodding your heads as you read this, thinking, *Of course we should cook for our pets, they deserve it.* But I'm also sure that most of you are going, *Uh-oh, he's officially lost his mind. That's just what I want to do—come home from a hard day's work and cook a three-course meal for my little Puff-Puff. That's why I didn't even have kids, because I don't want to do stuff like that!* I understand, believe me. Just hear me out, then I'll change the subject.

Marty's main point is that our animals should eat . . . hold on to your hats . . . *food.* Not plastic. Not ground-up bone. Not fecal matter or poisonous chemicals. Come on, if you're a cat lunatic, as we all are, that's hard to argue with. The right canned food is fine, and I definitely gave it to Norton from that point forward, but my attitude was that my cat was sick and why shouldn't I do *everything* I could to get and keep him healthy.

The answer was "no reason."

So I began cooking Norton's food.

Using Marty's formula, I whipped up concoctions that were about one-half meat or poultry and one-half grain and vegetable. I'd like to say that Norton gobbled it all down the second I placed it in his bowl, but that would be a total lie. What he did was sniff it suspiciously, much the way I would a steamed vegetable and brown rice platter at a health food restaurant, and then walk disdainfully away. But if my cat was the champion of stubborn, this was one instance when I was not going to give in to him. This was good for him and I was going to make sure he got healthy. It reminded me of the times my mother used to put my father on various diets, casually mentioning that he shouldn't be taking that second helping of potatoes, except that I couldn't make Norton feel guilty about his eating habits and I couldn't shove him in front of a full-length mirror so he could see that he was starting to resemble Jackie Gleason. He looked as dashing as ever and he seemed to feel fine, so he couldn't understand why his Twinkies were being withheld and being replaced by the equivalent of carrot juice. It was a battle of wills—but for the one and only time, it was a battle I was going to win. And I did. At first, Norton would pick out the good tidbits—the chicken or the meat—and leave the vegetables and grain (he was his father's son, after all; in a sick kind of way, I was proud of him for his tenacity). Then, after a few days, I noticed that some of the rice or pasta was gone. Just a little bit. And then, a few days later, more and more of it was consumed. Finally, miracle of miracles, the zucchini or the broccoli rape (Marty swore to me that his cats loved broccoli rape) were also gone. Pretty soon, Norton was licking his bowl clean. When he'd get canned food, on those occasions when I didn't have time to be the Emeril of cats, he did seem to eat with a little more gusto, but he definitely ate and got to like his homemade meals. While I'm on the subject, I should point out that these concoctions were definitely fit for human consumption (yes, I'll admit it right here and now— especially if I added a generous amount of garlic, I'd be unable to resist and would often share the exact same meal as my cat). It was also approximately the same level of difficulty as opening up a can. Once I knew Norton would consume the stuff, I'd make a big batch, enough to last a week, freeze some of it, and presto—instant healthy meals. The only bad moment I remember was when Janis came over one night and saw me chowing down on Chinese food that I'd ordered in. She shook her head—something she does a lot at my behavior, now that I think about it— and observed, "You're cooking for your cat but getting take-out for yourself? Don't you think there's something wrong here?"

The thing is, of course, I didn't think that. Eating my greasy shrimp with hot chili sauce and watching my cat scarf down his perfectly prepared chicken, rice and zucchini, I thought everything was exactly where it should be.

Now that Norton's health was stable and the food situation was taken care of, the next thing I needed to do was find another vet.

Yes, I know, I already had two—Turetsky and Marty; three if you count Dr. Pepper, which I certainly did—but I was only in Turetsky territory (Sag Harbor) on weekends during the nonsummer months, and not every weekend at that. And not only was Marty more of an advisor than my regular vet, he was a long drive away; it wasn't practical to consider using him on a regular basis or in case of emergency. So I began a Manhattan search.

Norton had actually been going to a vet in the city for quite a few years, but I didn't really think the guy was great. I'd stayed with him mostly because Norton had been healthy and this doctor did very little but give my traveling companion the occasional shot that was necessary for his overseas excursions. With all this going on, I decided I needed someone new. What pushed me over the edge was that I twice tried taking Norton in for his weekly dose of saline solution and both times we were kept waiting for two hours. There was no emergency, he'd just over-booked—much like a human doctor—and I thought this was not very considerate of either me or my cat. We began to look elsewhere.

People get very personally involved with their vets. If they're happy with their pet's treatment, they want every pet to have the same treatment. I noticed this when I was having a business lunch and, as most people did, at some point the woman asked me about Norton. I told her I was looking for a new vet in the city and she began raving about hers. He was the greatest, she said. He was fabulous, he was a genius. He was this, he was that . . . He was the first one I'd heard about, so I said I'd give him a try.

He was situated on the Upper East Side, which was totally inconvenient for me—especially if I had to go see him once a week for Norton's drip treatment—but inconvenience was not a deterrent when it came to caring for my cat. If I thought he was good and he was in Alaska, I would have taken Norton there. What *was* a deterrence was the fact that I *hated* this guy.

The first thing he did was tell me that Turetsky's treatment was all wrong. I didn't want to give the cat a big chunk of saline solution once a week, he said, I wanted to give him smaller portions three times a week. I explained that not only did I totally trust my Sag Harbor vet, I'd already had a second opinion, which totally matched Turetsky's, and this vet went into a total funk, as if I'd insulted him. When he asked me a few questions about Norton's health—and he didn't ask a lot of questions, he mainly gave me brusque answers, using a superior tone, letting me know how smart he was—I told him that I'd also been giving him supplements and herbs under the care of a holistic vet. He immediately sneered and said, "I don't believe in holistic medicine. It's a total sham." I told him that, while I wasn't totally sold, I thought it was doing the cat a lot of good. He told me I was completely wrong, that it was doing no good whatsoever. By comparison, when I told Turetsky and Dr. Pepper that I was seeing Marty, they were interested. They both had heard of him and what they each said was pretty much what I felt: that while there might not be enough empirical evidence to show that his methodology was completely sound, there was a hell of a lot of anecdotal evidence. They both asked about the supplements, jotted down the names so they could check them out on their own, and basically said, "Hey, it can't hurt. And if it helps, we're happy."

I was quickly losing patience with the East Side guy, but what really did it was when he began to examine Norton. He wasn't gentle.

I'd never been to a vet who didn't treat my cat as if he were something delicate and wonderful. Something special. This East Side vet handled Norton as if he were some kind of inanimate lump, twisting and turning parts of his body with no regard to the fact that Norton looked as unhappy as a cat can look. It reminded me of writing a script for a movie studio: you come up with a concept that might make a good film, do the best you can to create characters that people could conceivably care about and situations that seem real but can work on screen, and then some executive comes in and, without rhyme or reason, dumps all over it, ripping it to shreds. And worse, demanding rewrites that not only won't make it better but will, in fact, ruin it. Why? Because movie studio executives hate talent. They'd like to make films without the writers, directors or actors. Those films wouldn't be any good, but they'd sure be a lot easier for the executive and give him a lot fewer headaches. It's like a coach who insists that the athletes on his team conform to his system, rather than creating a system that works for the athletes' abilities. Same as the studio exec, that kind of coach hates talent. They want to be the star. They want the glory. At the very least, they want the credit.

I got the distinct feeling that this vet would have done very well in Hollywood or coaching the Knicks: he just plain didn't like his patients. He wanted their illnesses to fit his diagnoses. And he wanted their recoveries to match his treatments. If they didn't, well, screw 'em, he'd treat them the way he wanted to treat them anyway.

When he started rattling off a list of things I was going to do and not do for Norton, I interrupted him and said, "Excuse me, I don't think I'm going to do *any* of that. What I'm going to do is get the hell out of here." And that's exactly what we did. I apologized to my cat the entire way downtown and assured him I would do better. The only encouraging thing is the way Norton mewed at me from inside his shoulder bag—I knew he believed me.

I checked out a couple of other vets, and none seemed great, but then two sources converged and led me straight to the yellow brick road. Norton was in Turetsky's office for his weekly drip and I asked the aide there if she knew a good vet in the city. She told me that she'd worked for a wonderful woman, two wonderful women, in fact, at a place called the Washington Square Animal Hospital. I liked the name, since it meant it was close to my apartment in the Village. The idea of not having to take Norton seventy blocks in a taxi once a week was more than a little appealing. When I went back to the city, I called Ann King, Norton's fan who took such good care of him that one weekend Janis and I were away, to ask if she knew a good vet and she said, "Don't you know about the Washington Square Animal Hospital?" Seemed like fate. So I immediately made an appointment for the next day.

I didn't like Dr. Dianne DeLorenzo, the vet Norton and I met with at the clinic.

I *loved* her.

And so did Norton.

She immediately saw and understood the, as she called it, "stronger than usual" bond that existed between man and cat, and she seemed to get quite a kick out of it. She also picked up on the fact that Norton was different and unique (but remember our earlier lesson, class: not *very* unique), and best of all, when she examined him it was like watching someone treat royalty. There was none of that rough East Side jerk of a vet manner. This was someone who loved what she was doing and who cared immensely for her patients. She kept telling Norton how handsome he was, which, of course, made him extremely happy. And she even seemed pretty good with people. She didn't tell me how handsome I was, but she did manage to keep me calm and nonhysterical.

I confessed about my inability to give Norton his IV and she said she understood, then assured me that I could bring him in for that treatment whenever I wanted. I watched her give it to him herself that first session, and she was the perfect combination of gentle and firm. Norton didn't flinch when the needle went in and she let me hold him in my arms while he absorbed the fluid—her expertise and my loving stroke: the perfect combination for my cat. She also recommended someone named Yvette, a woman who used to work at the clinic, who would come to the apartment to do it if I ever needed that. What totally won me over was when I told Dianne I was also taking Norton for some holistic treatments. Her eyes lit up and she said that she was not trained in that area, knew very little about it, knew that a lot of people swore by it, and she was quite interested in learning more about it. She asked for Marty's phone number so they could speak and she could find out what, specifically, he was doing for Norton. Her attitude was "Maybe I'll learn something that will help me treat my patients better."

By the time I left her office, Norton not only had a new Manhattan vet, I was thinking of proposing marriage. What could be better for my catcentric life than being married to Norton's doctor? My fantasy was short-lived, maybe a minute or two—long enough for me to create a mental picture of my coming home to our snow-bound cabin in the woods to find Norton eating a hearty bowl of stew by the roaring fire and my new wife being serenaded by hundreds of happy, singing cats and dogs—since it turned out that Dianne was already happily married. Of course, for all intents and purposes, so was I, so that whole cabin–Dr. and Mrs. Schweitzer thing—or, rather, Dr. and *Mr.* Schweitzer thing—didn't really pan out. But the vet part turned out perfectly.

When Norton and I strolled out of the clinic and found ourselves on Ninth Street, we were both feeling pretty chipper. Once again, life was good. Everyone assured me that Norton was doing fine. Now it was time to wait and see what life brought us.

Of course, what life brought us was what life always brings.

Plenty of surprises.

CHAPTER 8

THE CAT WHO
STAYED HOME

B asically, things were normal. I was working away and Norton's kidney problem didn't seem to be slowing him down one iota. He was eating healthily and putting back on all the weight he'd lost, going in for his weekly shot (soon after our visit to Dr. DeLorenzo, everyone decided it was time for the shot to become twice weekly, so that's what we did), and finding new fans almost every day.

One of his big fans turned out to be a woman named Mary Bielaska, who was producing—along with her cat Zana, she announced—a CD of classical music she was calling *Classical Cats*. The idea, she said when she called to discuss it, was to pick songs that she felt were particularly catlike and that people could listen to with their feline pets at their side. She would also rename the familiar titles to make them more cat-friendly. One of the cuts, for instance, would be "The Sorcerer's Apprentice" by Paul Dukas, which, for the CD, would be retitled "Stalking Grass-hoppers." Another would be Johann Strauss's "The Beau-tiful Blue Danube Waltzes," renamed, for cat purposes, "A Feline's Fabulous Fantasy." I listened politely as Ms. Bielaska (the first time she called, I have to say I thought her name was Baked Alaska, which is why I was so willing to talk to her) described her scheme. While listening, I wondered why she was bothering to describe it to *me*. There was a reason, of course. And, as usual, it had nothing to do with me.

She wanted Norton to write the liner notes.

After some minor haggling—Norton was retired, after all—my cat and I came aboard (with me very much in the background).

For all his fans who have not had the pleasure of listen-ing to *Classical Cats: Music for Your Cat*, I now reproduce Norton's first and only literary dip into the record world (what you're missing out on, as well as the music, is that each CD came packaged with a small bag of catnip).

CLASSICAL CATS
Fe-liner Notes by NORTON

I was sitting in a cafe in Paris, oh, about a year ago now, sipping my usual *lait froid*—and a particularly delightful vintage it was. It was a lazy evening on the Left Bank. My human was occupied, paying scant attention to me, barely remembering to tell the waiter that I liked my *poulet roti* off the bone. Minding my own business, doing my best to ignore the rather large dog who, rudely and crudely, insisted on sniffing under my seat all through dinner, I couldn't help but notice a rather dashing feline sitting several tables to my left. He, too, seemed to be enjoying his *verre du lait*, so eventually we struck up a conversation.

We had quite a bit in common—we were both well traveled, we both thought the lamb at L'ami Louis to be the best on any continent, we were both quite a bit smarter than our owners—and we quickly became good and close friends. So I was not surprised when Zana—for that was my new friend's name—recently gave me a quick meow to tell me about his wonderful new idea for a CD. It was to be called "Classical Cats" and would be a compilation of classical gems that cats have long preferred. The genius of Zana's concept—aside from hiring that brilliant long-hair conductor Micetro Leopold Catscanini—is that he felt by putting all these classics in one collection, he could get human beings to upgrade their usual base taste and spend some time listening, learning and appreciating along with their feline companions. Zana, knowing my predilection for anything by Strauss and Debussy—known in my circles as Depussy—asked me to jot down a few words by way of introduction. Always one to favor the advancement of culture (After all, I'm the one who insisted my human finally stop writing those stupid books about how he tagged around with me all over the world!), I immediately agreed. *Et voilà.*

While Zana, for marketing purposes, had to include the human names for each composition (i.e., Offenbach's "Barcarolle" from *The Tales of Hoffman*), he quite properly has listed each masterpiece under its more appropriate and, I'm certain, original feline name. Thus that same "Barcarolle" becomes "The Butterfly Who Got Away," which, as all cats know, is what that particular orchestration is really about.

I can't quarrel with any of the selections herein (although I would have liked to see something included from Mozart's *Catting Around,* or as it's known to humans, *Don Giovanni*) nor with their well-thought-out order. Grieg's "Stretch and Yawn" is a gentle introduction to any cat's morning. I can't ever listen to these peaceful strains without envisioning myself on my human's pillow at 6 A.M., listening to him snore away, as—since it's clearly time he wake up to feed me—I cleverly stick my coldish nose in his eye and push it open. I also defy any self-respecting cat to listen to the next three selections without conjuring up that trio of life's great natural pleasures—running through and chewing upon a park's lush, green grass; bounding and leaping around a backyard in pursuit of a spindly grasshopper; and creeping up on a garden, thick with colorful, fragrant flowers, and doing one's best to pounce upon a butterfly fluttering just inches out of claw's reach.

Thrill to the heart-pounding excitement of Strauss's "The Dog Chase," then relax to the calming strains of Debussy's "To Purr With Love." Rev up again with the pulsating rhythms of "The Great Mouse Hunt"—can't you see yourself creeping across a sun-warmed linoleum floor, closer and closer yet to some delicious and unsuspecting furry little rodent?—and then luxuriate in the frivolity of Bizet's "To Chase a Tail." Surely, this genius must have had a tail of his own, carefully hidden from human view within the confines of his formal wear. How else could he see so clearly into our minds?

End this delightful concoction by wallowing in the sensuality of Strauss's waltz, then curl up by the fire—or just about anywhere else—and let your glowing eyes slowly close to Debussy's sweet-as-Pounce "Time for a Cat Nap." I myself like to play this one seventeen or eighteen times a day.

I could go on forever but Zana's only paying me three cans of Sheba and a personalized litter box, and even we Scottish Folds have to make a living. So, in closing, let me wish all you classical cats out there your own ball of string, a human to scratch you under the chin, a nice desk lamp to sunbathe under, and an evening listening to Zana's wonderful collection. Happy purring.

The *Classical Cats* experience was unique, in that most of Norton's fans—who kept in steady touch with him over the years—did not want him to do anything for them. They wanted to do things for him.

Gifts never stopped arriving. And I don't mean little cans of Pounce. I mean *gifts*.

One woman knew that Norton liked to zip around town in a shoulder bag (the weird thing is, when people either called or wrote to tell me stuff like this, they never said, "I read that Norton likes to zip around in his shoulder bag," they always said things like, "I know that Norton likes . . ." or, "I heard that Norton likes . . ." as if he told them himself. I never pursued this with them, I guess because I always thought it was possible that somehow he *had* told them, and I decided ignorance was bliss). So this woman sent a very colorful and comfortable shoulder bag—one that she'd hand knitted herself.

Clothing came fairly regularly. Sweaters, shirts, and for some reason, caps. I even got a tie, which I assume was for me because it was longer than Norton. It came from someone in Germany and it had big images of Norton painted all over it—one of him in front of the Eiffel Tower, one of him carrying a suitcase, one of him looking at what appears to be a menu—and on the back of the tie were printed the words "Norton is everywhere!" Luckily, we didn't receive any more angel outfits. One was enough. I used to have weird fantasies about some of this cat clothing. Outside of a church in Sag Harbor, there's a bin which the church uses to collect clothing that they disperse to people who need it. I regularly give them my old clothes, knowing they'll get to people who can really use them, but I was always tempted to toss in one of Norton's handmade sweaters. I just liked the idea of some woman sorting through the piles and coming upon a perfectly made, crocheted sweater that was one foot long and had four holes for arms.

Norton also received a lot of photos during his retirement years. People would send pictures of themselves, their cats, their cats' urns—yes, I swear—their houses, their cars (honest, one woman sent a photo of her car so Norton could see what he'd be chauffeured around in if he decided to come pay her a visit). He also was mailed a lot of poems (usually about cats and cat-related obsessions, but I have to say not always; some people just thought he'd enjoy regular poetry), books (occasionally published by a mainstream publisher, more often self-published, sometimes compiled just for Norton and hand bound), and then many useful items such as food (an English fan periodically sent him rabbit-flavored cat treats) and water bowls, beds, blankets, cat passports, and a wide variety of toys.

A lot of people tried to meet him, too.

For the most part, I'm pretty friendly to Nortonphiles. After all, I'm partly responsible for making people like my cat, so when they do indeed want to express their admiration for him, who am I to blow them off? I respond to almost every letter (except the ones telling me I'm speeding on my way to rot in hell for eternity) and I'm even usually polite on the phone when strangers call me up to talk cat stuff (Although, I must say, I don't like that too much; it's a bit audacious to call someone at home, in my opinion. It's why only my office number is listed now, not my home phone). But one time Norton, Janis and I were in Sag Harbor, relaxing on a sunny summer Sunday, when we got a phone call from someone and the conversation went exactly like this:

Man on Phone: Hello, is this Peter Gethers?

Me (suspicious; immediately recognizing that familiar cat-nut tone to the voice): Who's calling, please?

Man on Phone: My name's Bob Flayman (name changed to protect the cat insane). My wife and I are big fans of Norton's and we're trying to reach the same Peter Gethers who wrote those wonderful books.

Me (still suspicious, but warming to the words "wonderful books"): Yes, this is Peter.

Man on Phone: Oh great. I'm sitting in the car with my wife, we're just a couple of blocks away from you and we wanted to come over and meet Norton.

Me: What?

Man on Phone: We're in Sag Harbor and we're very close by, so we thought we'd come say hello.

Me: What?!

Man on Phone: We're big, big fans and—

Me: How do you know where I live?

Man on Phone: Well, you write about Sag Harbor, so we asked a few people and someone told us the name of the street, but we can't find—

I think I'll end the conversation here because I'm afraid, from this point on, I wasn't very polite to this guy and his wife. I explained that it was a Sunday and we were taking it easy and the idea of total strangers stalking my cat and paying a visit was a nightmare right out of "The X-Files" as far as I was concerned. I think I terrified the poor guy. When I hung up, I felt a little guilty and asked Janis if I'd overreacted. She agreed with my basic premise—stalking strangers are bad—but thought I could have been a little subtler. I felt particularly guilty because a few months later, Norton and I actually met these people. We were making a bookstore appearance in Manhattan and a really nice couple came up to us and said that they were the "nuts" who'd called us in Sag Harbor. They couldn't have been more pleasant, and clearly weren't stalkers *or* nuts, they were just two people who were touched and moved and entertained by the things they'd heard about my cat and wanted to see him for themselves. Hard to argue with, really. So I gave them some time with their favorite Fold and, judging by his purring and contented look, Norton gave them a favorable report.

But my favorite thing of all was when I got word in the early part of 1999 that Norton was being inducted into the Feline Hall of Fame. I got a letter asking me if I had any objection to Norton receiving such a prestigious honor, I wrote back and said no, of course not, then the next thing I knew, a fake scroll came in the mail—in case you're wondering what a fake scroll is, it's a piece of cardboard that has a scroll printed on it so the whole thing seems a lot fancier than it is—that said:

HALL OF FAME
Congratulations

NORTON—
The Cat Who Went To Paris

has been inducted
into this year's Hall of Fame
at the Diamond Level
by

Int'l Scottish Fold Association
This is in honor or memory of
CFA cats and catteries who
have enriched our lives.

They invited us to come to the induction ceremony (I think it was taking place in Florida) but I politely declined.

For one thing, it was a long trip to make and I figured that if they didn't even pop for a real scroll, they were hardly going to spring for the airfare. For another, I couldn't escape certain images that kept popping into my brain about who'd actually be attending a ceremony at the Feline Hall of Fame. I had visions of people dressed up in Garfield suits. And humans who'd had plastic surgery to fold their ears so they'd match their cats. When I started dreaming of the big Saturday night banquet—a long table, no utensils, bowls that had our first names stenciled on them and all the dry food we could eat—I knew it was best to stay away.

All in all, Norton took this sort of fanfare in stride. He was happy to be left alone—or, more accurately, to be left alone with me—but he was pleased, too, when people would fawn all over him. None of that changed during this period. The only thing that really did change after we got word of his kidney disease, is that he stopped traveling the way he used to (the most important reason why he missed his Hall of Fame induction).

The thing about kidney failure is that Norton didn't just drink a lot more, and he didn't just need to get his IV drip on a regular basis, he also urinated a lot more than he ever had before. You don't need to know the details—I'll let him keep his dignity, just as I hope no one ever talks about how many times I have to pee if *my* kidneys ever start to go, or any other time in my life now that I think about it—but he was using that litter box as it had never been used before. So I didn't think it was fair or healthy for him to go for long plane rides where no litter box was available. He'd had a great ride—literally—and all I cared about now was making his middle and old age as easy as possible for him.

This certainly made me revise my thinking when it came to my own travel, no question about it. For years, I could just pick up and go wherever and whenever I wanted, knowing that I could always take my best bud along with me. Now, I thought twice about leaving home by plane (driving was no problem—as far as Norton was concerned, a litter box on the floor of the back seat of the car was just as good as being at our apartment). For one thing, I had to make sure that Norton got his drip twice a week. This was crucial and it was a lot easier for me to be with him to make sure it got done. If I had to be away for business, Janis either took him to the vet or the woman Dianne DeLorenzo recommended, Yvette, would show up on the appointed morn and do what needed to be done in Janis's apartment. Mostly, I stayed close to Norton, though. I never said it out loud, since I thought it did sound just the tiniest bit weird, but I preferred being with him so I could make sure he was well taken care of. The curtailing of the travel didn't really bother me. It mostly meant Christmasing in Sag Harbor instead of Goult, which was hardly the end of the world.

It was a small sacrifice to make. And the fact is, I didn't consider it a sacrifice. If it meant spending time with him, I was more than happy to accommodate my cat's new schedule.

In addition to feline-related matters, quite a few things were happening in the human world, too, during this period.

Janis started her own successful business. She became,

and is now, a literary agent. It was a gutsy thing to do—striking out on one's own without a safety net is always somewhat terrifying—but it worked out well. Recently, she even sold a big novel about a guy's relationship with a cat. Several publishers were convinced I had written it under a pseudonym, but it wasn't me, I swear. In fact, one of the reasons this writer picked Janis is that when he first met her he said, properly cowed, "You're Norton's mother, aren't you?"

My mom also did a gutsy thing: she moved back to New York City after over thirty years in Los Angeles. She'd had it with the earthquakes and the driving. Plus, most of her family—her brother and three sisters and many nieces and nephews—were there, and, at age seventy-five, she was just plain in the mood for an adventure. My mother is big on adventure. A year or so earlier, she'd been on safari in Africa and had a stroke. In her tent, in the middle of the night, in the middle of the jungle. She had to walk a mile or two, hop on a raft and get towed across a river, get in a small plane, fly to London where she spent the night, then fly on to New York. When she arrived, she called me and said that she must have picked up a virus because the right side of her body was paralyzed. I called Janis and said, "Does this sound like a virus to you?" and Janis said, "Get her to the hospital, she's had a stroke!" Sure enough, that's what it was. She totally recovered, I'm happy to say, and, while I'm sure she would disagree, I thought the whole experience was almost worth it just to see the expressions on the various nurses' faces when they heard the part about walking two miles through the jungle.

One of the appealing things about my mom returning to the city of her birth (don't worry, Mom, one of the *many* appealing things) was that we now had a baby-sitter—excuse me, cat-sitter—for Norton when needed. It meant that, when necessary, Janis and I actually could go away for a couple of days and know that Norton was in good hands. And we did take advantage of this grandmotherly convenience from time to time. Norton quite enjoyed visiting with my mother. He ate well, there were some excellent nooks and crannies to prowl in her East Side apartment, and she had some pretty interesting dinner parties, which, of course, he attended. One of the appealing things for my mom about returning to New York—other than the mere fact that it wasn't the jungle—was getting to spend more time with her sister Belle, she of the scotch Hurricane fame. Unfortunately, that appeal didn't last very long because three months after my mother moved here, Belle died from a brain tumor.

She was eighty-three years old, which ain't too shabby, but it still felt like it was way too young because she was so vital and funny, so interested in the things around her and so very entertaining to be around. I was asked to deliver one of the eulogies at Belle's funeral. I agreed to do it and spoke about how, truth be told, Belle was kind of ordinary. She didn't discover the polio vaccine or reinvent the wheel or change the face of the planet. But I went on to talk about how funny she was, and honest, how protective she was of the people she loved, and how I didn't know anyone who was even remotely as generous. I said that I didn't believe that it was actually possible to bring back someone from the dead, but that I was reserving my judgment when it came to Belle, until I went out to dinner with my mother to see whether or not a ghostly vision with thinning hair came down from above to pick up the check.

I talked about how Belle managed something that most people never manage. Most people don't get better as they get older—they just get older. Belle actually managed to grow. She went to new places, tried new things, made new friends, got more sophisticated. I said she was a lot more interesting at eighty than she was at forty. And she was a better person—kinder, more understanding, softer. When you added all that up, I observed, that wasn't so ordinary. It was pretty amazing. I ended by saying that Belle realized that what counted in life was having a sense of humor and a sense of adventure and sharing those two things with the people you loved.

What I remember most about delivering that eulogy is that what should have been a five-minute talk took me about three hours to get through because every sentence or two I had to stop speaking so I could sob and blubber beyond belief. I was mortified that I couldn't keep hold of my emotions for a measly few minutes but there you have it. I couldn't. It's a good thing to remember, so you don't ask me to speak at your funeral. My other main memory came after the whole thing was over, when the entire Spring Trip Group—all of whom came to the service—went out for a drink at the nearest bar. We ordered an extra glass of scotch, put it in the middle of the table, and toasted Belle. Our toast was: "To the youngest person we know." At every one of our Spring Trips since then, we always order a glass of scotch and raise our glasses to my mother's sister.

The reason I'm telling you this sad story is not because I feel compelled to jerk a few tears. It's because what happened after Belle's death is both interesting and relevant.

What happened is that my mother, at age seventy-five, realized that she didn't care all that much for certain members of her family. No, it's not that she didn't care for them—she loved them dearly—they just weren't what she thought they were. For her entire life, they were more symbols than people. There was The Brother Who Was The Head Of The Family After Pop Died. There was The Clever Nephew With The Get-Rich Schemes, The Devoted Son, The Good Kid Who Was Taking Over The Family Business. Those images existed partly because that's the way Belle presented them to us (protecting them, since that was her role, but also I think that she genuinely believed in those images; that was her religion—family). But suddenly Belle wasn't around and my mother had to see beyond the images and what she saw was that they weren't at all what they were supposed to be. They weren't kind or generous or brave or even particularly nice, most of them. There were exceptions, of course (note: this is a good writer's trick; now every one in the family can read this and decide that he or she is obviously one of the exceptions).

What I think happened was that with Belle gone, the glue that held everyone together was also gone. Minus that glue, it ceased to be a family unit, becoming instead a group of individual personalities. And looked upon as individuals rather than as a family, well . . . it wasn't a pretty picture. In fact, if you count some of my cousins' hairpieces, the picture was *really* grotesque. They did what people always seem to do when the strongest among them disappears: they got petty, they got small, they got greedy and, worst of all, they got mean. In a sense, it was horrible for my mom. She lost the one family member she was closest to—her sister Belle—but she also lost most of the others. By choice, yes, when she had her moment of clarity, but they were still lost.

I know someone whose father died several years ago (his mother had died a few months earlier). He was at the hospital with his dad when the final moment came, and he called his sister to tell her the sad news. He told her that he'd have to stay at the hospital for an hour or so, to take care of the paperwork and other details, then he'd go back to the parents' home, which is where he was staying while he was in town. He got back there just in time to see his sister driving away—having taken all the paintings and other valuables that she wanted out of the house. Almost every family I know has stories like that. I've seen and heard dozens of them. Someone important to the family structure dies, others in the family revert to their neurotic (and usually greedy) worst instincts. It's what death often does to families. It breaks them apart.

As my mother saw her long-held image of her family crumble, she could have done one of two things: she could have crumbled herself, which so many people do, or she could have moved on and picked her own "family." Luckily, she did the latter. Even luckier, her new coterie included some *real* family members—me, my brother, my brother's son (I should probably have listed the grandkid, Morgan, first since he's far and away the fave), Janis, Belle's daughter Beth, Lil (another of my mother's sisters), some other nieces and nephews. In addition, there were many close friends who made the cut; people she trusted and loved. Few people are capable of making this sort of transition at any age. At my mom's age, it's particularly admirable. Of course, she's no stranger to admirable life changes. She also started her career when she was in her early fifties. Now she's written eight or nine cookbooks (including a chocolate book that was *Food and Wine Magazine*'s pick for the very best cookbook published in the year 2000) and is still going strong. She's quiet on the outside but inside she's strong enough to not only make choices, she's determined enough to stay the course once those choices are made.

I think choice is preferable in just about any situation, particularly when it comes to who you wind up trusting and loving. It's worked fairly well for me, too. I've had the same best friend since I was eight years old. Most of my other good friends I've held on to for years. Janis you already know all about. And, of course, most of all there was Norton.

Most of my friends are real friends. I feel like they could call me up and ask me to do just about anything and that I could do the same. If you don't feel that way about friends or your chosen family, my attitude is "what's the point?" I tend to push people away at the beginning, but if they get through the radar, once they're in, they usually stay. And that's the reason I wanted to talk about Belle's death. Because thinking about her life, seeing the impact her death had on my mom, giving the eulogy and focusing in on what was important, all served to hammer home the fact that I was pretty happy with the family I'd picked for myself. I felt like I'd made the right choices.

And then, in the year or so after Belle died, a few things happened, as they always do, and a few more choices had to be made.

Some peripheral friends fell by the wayside. A longtime friendship fizzled. There were a couple of divorces and sides eventually were chosen. I wrote a best-selling thriller under a pseudonym, got a chunk of money, spent time with my cat in Washington Square Park and used that money to buy my (and his) dream apartment, right near the dog run.

In the few months it took to fix up the apartment, Norton and I alternated living between Sag Harbor and Janis's apartment. In Sag Harbor, I took him to Turetsky for his twice weekly shots. In the city, that wonderful woman Yvette came to administer his treatments.

Then all the contracting work was done and I was on the verge of moving in. I was absolutely ecstatic. There we were, Norton and I, about to take over a gorgeous apartment, overlooking the park, steps away from his favorite spot in the entire city.

Finally it came: moving day.

Life was perfect.

And then I had to rethink all my choices and all my thoughts on family and what was and wasn't important. I even had to rethink the *concept* of choice.

Because on the day I moved into my dream apartment, I found out that my cat had cancer.

CHAPTER 9

THE CAT WHO
HAD A WILL
TO LIVE

What Norton had developed was a slow-growing, low-grade lymphoma in his liver.

I knew this because after doing so well with his kidney failure for so long, he began to lose weight. Even though he was eating to his heart's content. He'd also begun to throw up more than usual (I know, I know, how can you tell with a cat? But I could tell, believe me). So I took him in to see Dianne DeLorenzo and she looked concerned, ran some tests, then she called me first thing in the morning—while I was standing in my brand new living room—and told me about the cancer.

It was a fairly similar situation to my session with Dr. Turetsky when I heard about the kidney problem. My new vet told me that there were many things that could be

done, that we'd caught it very early, that this did not necessarily mean what she was sure I thought it meant. I told
her I understood all that and I did, I really did, but when I
hung up the phone, I picked Norton up and cradled him in
my arms, kissed him on top of the head, told him I loved
him about twenty times, and I bawled like a little baby until I absolutely couldn't cry anymore.

When I decided I was composed, I made a few instant
decisions.

One was to call Janis and tell her. That's when I found
out I wasn't all that composed because I think what I actually said was, "Well, Dr. DeLorenzo called and . . ." And
that was it. Then it was another crying jag. Janis waited me
out very patiently. When I could finally speak, I tried again,
didn't do a whole lot better, but I did manage to convey the
gist of the situation. She asked if I wanted her to leave work
and come over, but I said no, that I was fine, I just needed
to get used to the idea. Truer words were never spoken. I
did in fact need to get used to the idea that my beloved cat
was not sick now, he was dying.

The second decision was one I couldn't implement for
another hour. That was when Yvette came over to give
Norton his IV drip.

Yvette was a terrific person, a black woman who had
worked for several vets, loved animals, and was incredibly
good with Norton. She cooed things like "pretty boy" and
"sweet baby" at him and he was a sucker for that.
Periodically, when she came, she tried to show me how to
do the dastardly thing myself. Even though it would cost
her money, she kept telling me that it would be much nicer
for my cat if he were receiving the treatment at my hands.
Every time she'd tell me this and then show me what to do,

I knew she was right—but I still couldn't bring myself to do it.

Except this was my second decision. My cat was now genuinely ill and, much to my shock, one of the first things that ran through my mind was that I wanted to be the one to take care of him. I didn't want to be distant or disconnected. And I didn't even want things to be nonmessy and safe. I wanted to do whatever needed to be done and I wanted to start doing it immediately.

So when Yvette walked in the door, I told her that Norton had cancer and that I wanted to start giving him the IV. I also told her not to tell anyone—not about my out-of-character decision, about the cancer. I know it might sound silly, but I didn't want people to know. As weird as it seems, I wanted to give Norton a little more privacy. He wasn't like normal cats—people not only asked me about him constantly, people drove hundreds of miles to meet him! When I'd have dinner with friends, they would almost always ask me how Norton was doing, if he'd been anywhere good lately, if he was up to anything special. It was a little like having a teenaged son. A *precocious* teenaged son. People were very curious about almost every detail of his life and I knew that would include his illness. I believed Dianne when she told me that he was in no immediate danger, that he was not going to die right away, so as always, I did for him exactly what I would have done for myself: I kept quiet, so he could go on leading as normal a life as possible and not have people feeling sorry for him.

I paid Yvette but told her I was going to do things myself today. She began to set up the drip so she could show me how to do it. I told her it was unnecessary. She'd shown me plenty of times, I understood exactly what had to be done. I just had to go ahead and do it. She then stepped back and waited but I told her she didn't have to stick around, I wanted to do this by myself. She didn't look thrilled with this decision, but I knew that I'd never be able to do it with someone watching. This was between me and my cat. It was personal.

So Yvette left, shaking her head (Hmmm, do you sense a theme running through my life?) and there I was, alone with Norton and that damn plastic bag.

I'd seen Yvette do this very often, so I followed her example. She always did it in the bathroom. It was a small, confined space, which made it easier for her and, she said, made Norton more comfortable. It was easy to attach the bag so the liquid flowed easily, and one could sit comfortably. Made sense to me. So no more dining room table for the Kid. I put the bag in the bathroom sink, which was filled with hot water, to warm up the liquid. Then I hooked the whole contraption up to the rod that held the shower curtain. So far so good. I still stuck with the pink needles—yes, it would take longer but I wasn't confident that I'd get one of those giant green suckers into my cat without killing him (or me). I hooked up the tube, got the needle ready, put Norton in my lap exactly the way I'd seen Yvette do it. Then I leaned over and whispered for a minute or two in his little folded ear. Not just nonsense babble, either. I said that I really loved him, that I'd never hurt him, and I asked him to please, please, please be good and not to run away while I did this, even if I didn't do it perfectly, because it was really important and I needed his help.

Did I really and truly think he understood me?

Well . . .

Well . . . *yes.*

Okay, damnit, I admit it! *I did.* Honest to god. I was totally, 100 percent convinced he knew exactly what I was saying.

And I still think so.

Because here's what Norton did. I gathered his skin up between the thumb and two forefingers of my left hand, just as I'd been taught, put the needle in (I heard a tiny little pop that let me know I'd done it successfully) flicked the switch so the liquid began flowing through the tube and into his body, and the entire time my cat sat there and purred his little head off.

After about thirty seconds, I relaxed. I didn't realize I'd been quite so tense but I guess I was because it was like coming out of a trance. I realized that I was sitting in my bathroom, a purring cat on my lap, and I'd done what I'd been dreading doing for a year and a half. I began to pet Norton, firmly stroke his side and then his head while the solution flowed into him, and I kept telling him what a wonderful guy he was. I thanked him profusely and when I did—I'm not kidding now—he meowed in response. A soft, gentle meow. Just one, so I knew it was a specific answer. And now I have to tell you that not only am I sure he understood what I'd been saying, I'm positive I understood what *he* was saying.

He was saying: *thanks.*

After that, it was easy as pie. In fact, these sessions weren't just chunks of time I managed to get through, they were blocks of time I genuinely looked forward to. As time progressed, Norton needed the drip more than twice a week. Eventually, he needed it every day. And every single day, they were my favorite ten minutes in that day. We'd go into the bathroom, close the door. Norton would nestle on my lap, purring the moment he was snuggled into the proper position. While he purred, I spoke to him, telling him how great he was, how much I liked him. Then I'd slip the needle in—eventually I even got comfortable using the large green suckers instead of the little pink ones; hey, I was a pro—and he'd purr even louder. We'd sit for five minutes while the soothing liquid flowed into him. While sitting, I'd talk more, he'd purr, occasionally meow in response. Sometimes he'd lick my hand and bury his nose into the crook of my arm. There was never a time I sat there with him when I didn't have the warm feeling that we were both where we wanted to be, doing what we wanted to be doing, which was spending time together and making him feel better.

Here's the other thing I'm absolutely positive of:

Norton was helping me. He knew how nervous I was. He understood how afraid I was of hurting him and screwing up. He understood how worried I was about him. So he helped me. He didn't just stay calm, he went out of his way to be friendly, to show me that what I was doing was okay, that the whole situation was okay. He understood that I was helping him—the daily liquid clearly made him feel healthier and happier; I could see it within seconds of starting the drip process—so he did the same for me. Noncat people might not believe me (although any noncat person who's reading this book has got to be pretty weird, so he or she might believe me at that), but I'll bet when the letters start rolling in after this book is published, I'm going to get a lot of similar stories of cats guiding their owners through difficult situations. And even if I don't, I *know* that Norton took me through the process and showed me how to do it. Showed me that I *could* do it.

I was used to Norton being such a good teacher. He'd imparted valuable life-lessons—forcing them through my thick skull—his entire life.

What I wasn't expecting was just how great a teacher he was.

And what I didn't realize was that the lessons were just beginning.

The next thing I had to deal with was treatment. This went beyond the subcutaneous drip I was finally administering for his kidney failure. This was cancer, after all. This was serious.

I went in to meet with Dianne, who did a good job explaining what was happening to my cat's body. She showed me the results of the blood tests: what was high or low, what was still normal, what was dangerous and had to be closely monitored. She also had done a needle biopsy which confirmed the diagnosis of lymphoma and said that all signs indicated that the cancer had not spread beyond the liver. This was good news. But she also said that I needed to see an animal oncologist. It was the first I knew of such a profession but I said I would willingly make an appointment. Dianne said that it was likely Norton would need chemotherapy.

When Norton and I got home—to get from the Washington Square Animal Hospital to our new apartment we had to walk right through Washington Square Park and past the dog run, so this became our regular routine: going to the vet, Norton in his shoulder bag; stopping on the way back to sit among and check out the frolicking canines—I called Marty Goldstein. I told him about Norton's cancer and, as always, he was not just calm he was extremely comforting. He stressed that what he said might sound odd but that the kidney problem was relatively stable, so other than the cancer Norton was healthy. His appetite was good, everything else was functioning, and the cancer was contained in one small area. "Norton feels good, doesn't he?" Marty asked. I looked at my cat, who was curled up happily next to me on my desk and I said that yes, he felt really good. Marty then told me he was going to talk to Dianne and get her to fax him the results of all the latest tests, then he wanted me to bring Norton up to see him. He'd had extraordinary success treating cancer in animals, as I well knew, and he told me not to worry. He said that the odds were that Norton had a relatively long life ahead of him. There was no need to panic. When I told him about making an oncologist appointment, he told me that was exactly the right thing to do, but he also said that I should talk to him before making any commitment to treatment.

The next day, I took my cat uptown—to the Upper *West* Side this time—and we went to the cat oncologist.

Remember my unpleasant interlude with the East Side rich cat vet? Well, this was even more unpleasant. I stood by while Norton went through a battery of tests, mostly with nurses, and then the doctor himself came in. He was perfectly nice and recognized both how nervous and upset I was. He gave me some literature to read, pamphlets that explained exactly what cancer was and what the various treatments were, and then he explained to me about the chemotherapy. It was to be administered via shot once a week, as I recall, for six or seven weeks. And before the shots commenced, Norton was to immediately start taking something called prednisone twice a day for two weeks. I tried to ask reasonably intelligent questions but I was in that nether land where nothing seemed quite real. I do remember asking two questions, however. One, would the shots make my cat sick? And two, what would they actually accomplish? In other words, Was I going to be ruining my cat's life just to keep him alive? And if so, for how long would he actually be *kept* alive?

I also remember the doctor's answers very clearly. He explained to me that chemo on cats doesn't cause the same side effects it does on people. He said that Norton would not get ill from these shots. Not at all. And then he said that with the shots, Norton could live as long as nine months. Without them he'd definitely be dead in two months.

Excuse me?

Those were my exact words. It was all I could manage to get out of my mouth.

And he repeated what he said, unemotionally, a throwaway: If I gave him the chemotherapy treatment, my cat had nine months, tops. Without it, it was absolutely certain he couldn't live more than another eight weeks.

I started stammering: "But . . . but . . . but . . . Dr. De-Lorenzo said he could live quite a wh-wh-while." I started to explain that Marty Goldstein even said the cat was fairly healthy other than the cancer but it sounded kind of ridiculous coming out of my mouth.

The oncologist shrugged and said, "It's your choice.

You can do what you want." It was as if he lost interest the second I hinted that I was questioning whether or not I'd go for the chemo. "All I'm saying is that if you don't do it, your cat'll be dead very soon."

That was the end of the consultation. Except that he told me I should make up my mind quickly. If I waited more than a few days, it would be too late.

When I left his office, I felt as if I'd been hit over the head with a sledgehammer. And needless to say, my trip back downtown with Norton was not a happy one.

The second I walked in the door, I called Marty. He calmed me down, talked me out of my hysteria and told me to bring Norton up to his clinic the next morning. Before hanging up, he said, "Hey, I told you not to worry and I meant it. Your cat's going to live quite a while yet."

Not worry?

Oh sure. No problem. Dr. Frankenstein had just told me I had two months left with my favorite creature on earth and I wasn't supposed to worry? Right.

Do I have to bother to say it? I spent the rest of that day and night doing *nothing* but worrying. Then Norton and I got up bright and early the next morning and drove to South Salem.

Marty did his usual gentle poking and probing with Norton, elaborated on a few of the things I'd already heard about his latest tests, x-rays and biopsies, and then said, "It's like I told you. Your little buddy's got cancer—but other than that, he's pretty healthy."

"But the oncologist," I started to moan. "He said—"

And then Marty Goldstein said nine wonderful words: "Doctors are not gods. Sometimes we get things wrong."

I didn't realize you were allowed to say that about doctors. Once the realization sunk in that you were, boy, was I happy.

Marty then went on to elaborate. What he said was that it was certainly a viable option to put Norton on the chemotherapy cycle. He was very reasoned about it and said that it definitely could and probably would help. But he also said that contrary to the oncologist's assertion, there was at least a fifty-fifty chance that the treatment would make Norton sick, to a lesser degree than it would with a person, but sick nonetheless. Marty said that I couldn't make the wrong choice—whichever way I went would be correct. When I asked what he would do, he said that if Norton were young, say five or six, rather than fourteen, he'd give him the chemotherapy. His system could withstand it and it could conceivably knock out or at least slow down the cancer. But at Norton's age, the question was, was I going to go for quality or quantity. He said he could keep Norton healthy and happy for a fairly long time without poisoning him, which is essentially what chemo does. My wonderful, perfect cat wasn't going to live forever, Marty made sure I understood that. But he was not—repeat, *not*—in immediate danger. He was not going to live for just two more months. In fact, Marty doubted very much that the oncologist's nine-month projection was his limit. He said, again, that my pal was happy, felt good and had a genuinely strong will to live. Marty says stuff like that—things like one's cat has a strong will to live—and at first I thought he was pretty much full of it. But he wasn't. And in this instance he was as right as anyone could ever be.

He told me that he wanted to put Norton on an elaborate new system of supplements. He said that I should get blood tests on a regular basis with Dianne DeLorenzo, so we could monitor his progress. If I didn't like the way things were going, I could always go back and opt for the chemo (although Marty would never say this, my interpretation was that the oncologist was full of shit when it came to that, too: there was no reason I had to make my decision overnight). And then Marty said that he wanted to put Norton on a two-day continuous supplement drip to flush out his entire system. I asked how I could keep him on an IV for forty-eight hours and he said that I didn't have to, I was going to leave Norton with him. I started to protest, but he said it was important. He also said he wouldn't leave Norton alone in the clinic overnight—he'd take him home with him.

I took a deep breath, decided I felt a little bit like I was sending my cat off to Mexico to get treated with apricot pits, and said okay. I bit my lower lip to keep from sobbing again, kissed Norton goodbye, got in my car and drove back to the city.

For two days, I paced around my apartment, went to the dog run by myself and felt like an idiot, and worried like crazy. The first night, I called Marty at home to see how Norton was doing. The report came in: Just fine. And he was getting along with Marty's various cats and dogs like gangbusters. In fact, it was going so well, Marty wanted to keep him for one extra day. "Really," he said. "Trust me."

At the end of the seventy-two-hour period (and yes, in case you're wondering, I did call a couple of more times to check on my cat's progress; well, okay, more than a couple—I called about ten times), I headed back upstate and picked Norton up. Naturally, he had totally charmed everyone in the clinic. They were not at all happy to see me, knowing I was there to take him away.

Marty told me the treatment went well. With a big smile, he instructed me to take Norton back to Dianne and, in twenty-four hours, to get another blood test. After that, he said, I should start the new program of supplements and vitamins and get a blood test every three to four weeks.

I said okay, drove back to the city, petting my cat—who, I have to admit, looked particularly healthy and perky—the entire way, and made an appointment at the Washington Square Hospital.

When I got to her office, I told Dianne that I'd made my decision. I was going to see how Marty's treatment went and, for the moment, I was going to pass on the chemo.

I don't think she approved, but she was very understanding. She, too, said I could change my mind at any time. She even said that she could administer the chemo shots, if that would make me more comfortable, as long as the oncologist prepared the proper dosage. I said that it would indeed make me more comfortable, but at the moment I was going to see how this played out without it. I had thought long and hard about this. I really tried to keep it in perspective and I kept telling myself I was talking about a cat, not a world leader or a relative or even just a regular, normal human being. Nonetheless, perspective be damned, I felt as if this were one of the most important decisions I'd ever had to make and I felt very strongly that I had to trust my instincts. And my instincts were, overwhelmingly, to go for quality over quantity. They were to go ahead and do what I'd done so far during all the years I'd spent side by side with my beloved little pal: give him the best possible life he could have, so when it ended there would be no regrets for either one of us.

Once before I'd been faced with a similar situation. When I'd gotten the word that my father was dying, I flew (actually, Norton and I flew together) to be with him. He was still in the hospital then and it looked pretty bad. His doctor pulled me aside and said that when the time came, if I saw my father was in too much pain or had passed the line where we thought his life was no longer worth continuing, he could do something about it. Lowering his voice, he said that he could increase the morphine drip, gradually put my father into a coma and . . . He trailed off but the end of the sentence, the words he didn't and couldn't say were, "and kill him." There was no question in my mind that it was a humane offer. And one I would jump at if it needed to be done. I thanked the doctor—who made it clear that, officially, we had not had the conversation— then I went and explained the situation to my mother and brother. My mom said that she felt it was the right thing to do if the time came when we thought he was suffering too much or if his brain stopped functioning. My dad had made it very clear that he did not want to stick around in any kind of vegetative state. But she also said that she couldn't be the one to do it. My brother was in total agreement but wasn't a hundred percent sure if he could do it, either. I knew that I could and I told them that. So we tacitly agreed that if things got worse, I'd tell the doctor and no one would ever know—including them.

Luckily, it didn't come to that. Just because I *could* do it didn't mean that I *wanted* to. My father perked up slightly, enough to let us know that he wanted to die at home, which is what he did a few days later—naturally, with no artificial acceleration.

I remembered that conversation as if it had happened yesterday and strangely enough, this situation with Norton was a more emotional decision for me. I was weirdly unemotional when talking to my father's doctor. I do know the difference between humans and animals, don't worry. I haven't totally crossed that line yet. But with my dad, it was a question of days, possibly even hours. And it was a question of relieving rather than prolonging the suffering. I didn't even think it was a difficult decision—it struck me as the *only* decision. Now, however, if the oncologist was to be believed, what I was doing was, by my gamble, possibly taking six months to a year from the life of the sweetest, gentlest, most genuinely loving creature I'd ever encountered. I didn't know what kind of suffering would be involved either with or without the treatment. I didn't have a clue. But I tried to think what I would have done for myself—and I realized I'd be doing exactly the same thing. I'd never actually faced up to this question before. Yes, I wanted to live as long as possible. No question about it. But that desire was not as powerful as my longing to live as well as possible. If it were me, I'd try for quality and I'd try for natural.

So that's the decision I made for my cat.

When I realized I'd made the right call was when Dianne called me the day she got the results of Norton's latest blood test.

"I don't quite know what to tell you," she said. I prepared myself for the worst, but that wasn't what she meant at all. "I don't understand it," she went on, "and I don't see how it's possible . . . but after whatever it was that Marty did up there with that drip, the results of Norton's blood test are exactly as if he'd had a very successful chemo therapy treatment."

Thus began my new stage as primary caregiver to a cat.

When we were out in Sag Harbor, I made a special trip over to see Drs. Turetsky and Pepper and I told them about the cancer. They were genuinely sad. I think their sadness stemmed partly from the fact that they were compassionate people and loved animals and they didn't like the idea of any of their patients getting cancer. But I also think there was something more going on, particularly with Turetsky who had treated Norton since he'd been a kitten. They had come to be attached to my cat. They liked him, and I think they recognized that elusive will to live, so part of their sorrow was personal. They didn't want to lose him. While I was there they asked about the treatment he was getting and I described everything that had happened so far. Naturally, they put themselves at Norton's disposal but during the next few months, we were mostly going to be in the city, so their contact would, at best, be on the occasional weekend.

Because we were spending more time in Manhattan, my wonderful new apartment soon took on the air of the emergency room at St. Vincent's Hospital. I had the IV drip bag hanging from my shower curtain at all times. In my pantry were several large Baggies filled with needles. Marty said that Norton needed to receive certain new supplements via hypodermic needle, so I had hypodermics lying around, too—and not only did I use them on my cat, I got pretty good at using them.

Feeding Norton was now nearly a full-time occupation.

When Marty sent me my latest box of supplements, it came with an official-looking sheet that had scribbling all over it and a box that explained the codes used so I could understand the scribbling. There were thirteen supplements, each one listed on the left of the sheet. If a liquid, it would indicate that I was to give two or three drops or a third or a half of a dropper. If it was a pill it would tell me to use the whole pill or half or a third (just for the record, it's really a lot of fun to try to chop tiny little pills into thirds!). If it was a powder, I'd get the dosage in teaspoons: a third, a quarter, a half. On the right of this piece of paper, and corresponding with each individual supplement, there were things written such as OD AM O/F. There were also things like BID and EOD and A/D. Thank God for the key code because, even with it, it took a lot of studying before I eventually figured out that OD meant that Norton was supposed to get that particular supplement once daily. BID was twice daily. TID was three times per day. EOD = Every other day. OCC was once or twice per week. A/D meant alternate days, O/A was orally alone, O/F was orally or with food. F/D told me I was supposed to follow the directions on the bottle and A/N was as needed.

So in addition to cooking his fish, chicken or shrimp with rice or pasta and fresh, green vegetables, my routine was as follows:

Every morning, as soon as we were both awake, I

would head into my pantry, pick out several small bottles, place Norton on top of the butcher block kitchen counter and give him half a dropper of something called Super Glandulars, which was described on the label as high-concentration 1050, liver and B-12 glandular. I also gave him half a dropper of something that Marty concocted that was simply labeled "kidney." I can't say Norton loved taking this stuff but he never complained, rarely even squirmed. I'd pet him, he'd open his mouth and in the stuff would go. Next, every morn, was Hepaticol Drops, four drops' worth. The label described this tasty brew as Homeopathic Endocrine Sarcode Combination HHD. Yum yum yum. Every other day (EOD if we remember our secret code) in the morning, Norton got two or three drops of Milk Thistle Seed. Each evening he was given different drops. His predinner warm-up was small doses of Renal Drops and D.A. Gland Formula 1010. For pills, in various combinations at various times during the day, he got Cod Liver Oil (softgels), some truly weird-sounding thing called Tang-Kuei 18, Lipotrope, Beta-Thyme, Hemaplex and a very foul-smelling Raw Kidney Concentrate which had to be crushed up into a powder. As if this weren't enough, he also got two additional powders mixed in with his meals, Psyllium Husks Powder and Vet-Zimes Formula V5. And I'm not done yet, because Marty gave me some additional pills that basically had many features of the chemotherapy treatment: Natural Cortisone. To top it all off, Norton was quite often nauseous, so Dr. Pepper gave me an antinausea prescription for something called Metoclopram while Marty provided the all-natural version. Both pills were a great help but even with them, for some periods of time Norton would throw up once or twice, even three times a day. This was practically the most heartbreaking thing of all for me, listening to him cough and choke and spit up, knowing there was nothing I could do but hold him and rub him and try to soothe him. Often, in the middle of the night, I'd hear him down on the floor, giving that little cough of his that I came to know so well. It meant he was struggling to get something out of his system. He never did it in bed—he'd always hop down on the floor and try to do it as discreetly as possible—so I'd swing myself out of the covers, find him, and spend five or ten predawn minutes petting him and talking to him to keep his spirits (and mine) up.

The hardest part of all this was getting my stubborn little friend to swallow pills. The drops were no problem, he took those like a champ. He wasn't wild about the various powders that went into his food, but eventually he'd get hungry and have to eat. But the pills. Damn, those were tough! If I cleverly tried to mix them in with his food, I'd come back to check when he was done eating and all the food would be gone—and the pills would be there in the middle of the bowl, licked clean but absolutely whole. If I tried to force them down his throat—and I was terrible at doing this; it's the one thing in which I never got even *close* to vet-level skills—I'd be positive he'd swallowed, go away satisfied, then an hour later I'd see the very same pills lying on the floor in the kitchen, where he'd somehow managed to not only spit them out but leave them in a very visible spot so I'd be sure to know that he'd outsmarted me. Eventually I was able to figure out a way to get them inside him 90 percent of the time. After all, I *was* the one with the larger brain (and if you believe that, I've got a uranium mine in Asbury Park I'd like to sell you). My trick was that I wrapped the pills in a tiny dab of peanut butter, which

Norton loved. It also was pretty amusing to watch him eat, because the stuff was so good but so sticky that he'd be licking his lips for half an hour afterward. Even with the peanut butter (either smooth or crunchy, he wasn't fussy), occasionally he'd still manage to spit the pills out, but not nearly as often.

My duties didn't end there, either. Every so often, I'd dip a syringe into a vial labeled Adrenal Cortical Extract and zap it into my very accepting cat.

If you're getting the urge to refer to me as Dr. Pete, I'll accept the moniker, because I was also becoming quite adept at reading Norton's medical charts. I had many conversations with Drs. DeLorenzo and Goldstein in which I would study the fax that one or the other had just sent me, then call and observe, "The hemoglobin count is a little low, don't you think?" or, "The phosphorus is right in midrange, that's a big improvement," or, "The creatinine level is still high but it's come down drastically from the last count, so I think things are going well. Maybe we should go OD instead of OED on the kidney drop." I started having lengthy conversations about lecithin deficiencies and digestive enzymes and bilirubin counts and many other things I'd never heard of or wanted to hear of a scant few months earlier.

The other thing that was kind of interesting is how Norton's illness was slowly but surely altering my own life and lifestyle.

I saw the effect of Norton's healthy diet on his behavior. I had come to believe that it was helping to keep him alive. It made sense. Take the poison out of his system, replace it with things that were nutritional and replenishing, naturally his body would be better able to fight off disease.

And that's exactly what happened. So I started doing the same thing. I mean, I didn't start inhaling heaping plates of Vet-Zimes Formula V-5 but I cut out a lot of the fake non-food we all consume on a regular basis and tried to think a bit more holistically, without becoming a nut about it. (Let's face it, who wants to live to 120 if we can't eat the occasional bucket of Popeye's fried chicken, garlic, onion and pepperoni pizza or, best of all, the chocolate caramel dessert thing at the Gramercy Tavern restaurant?) But, overall, I followed my cat's example and began to think that a sensible diet might actually be a good thing. As usual, though, I never should have mentioned this to Janis, who actually knows about most things medical. She, too, saw what was happening with Norton and it had the sobering effect on her of trying to save me the way I was trying to save him. As soon as I showed the slightest interest in my own health, I started getting a fax a day from her: newspaper articles talking about how tomatoes can effectively fight cancer, magazine articles detailing what vitamins to take to combat arthritis, lists of carcinogenic foods, essays on what herbs to take to keep one's vision from disintegrating into a blurry blob. Some of the suggestions I took, others I just *told* her I was taking so she'd stop nagging me, but didn't do a thing about. Generally, though, seeing what holistic treatment did for Norton made me accept it as a very viable way for humans to live.

I also had become much less *afraid* of sickness. And of the messy side of life.

If Norton threw up, and spasms racked his little body, I was more than happy to hold him and massage his throat until he was back to normal. I cleaned up after him constantly, sometimes all day long, because slowly and gradually he was becoming incontinent. At least two or three times a week, he didn't seem to make it to his litter box. But I didn't care. So eventually I'd have to get a new carpet (or couch or hell, even a new apartment), what difference did it make; the only thing I wanted was for his life to be enjoyable and pain-free. I liked feeding him all the weird supplements he was taking, I liked holding him when I gave him his shots, I even didn't mind wrestling with him to get those pills down his throat. It was contact, physical and emotional, and I am absolutely convinced that, even as his body was failing, he knew that this contact was bringing us closer and closer together.

I appreciated the time we spent together more than I ever did. We'd go for walks together or sit in the park almost every day. At home, Norton had always been independent. He was not a lap cat. He liked to keep an eye on me, and usually stay in the same room I was in, but he rarely came up and collapsed on my lap when I was reading or watching TV. Now, however, he seemed to want to be as close to me as I did to him. He was *always* by my side. When I was working, he napped on the desk next to my computer, inches from my touch. If I was relaxing on the couch, he'd hop on up and manage to slide in next to me, his body brushing against my thigh. In bed, he was back to sleeping right next to me on the pillow, which he hadn't done on a regular basis since he'd been a small kitten.

It was as if he were saying, *I trust you.* He knew that I understood what he was going through and somehow our roles had become slightly reversed. In all the years past, if I had the flu and felt rotten, Norton would always be there, providing a comforting presence and touch. When I had my shoulder operation and spent a few days in bed, moaning and groaning and not being able to move, he never left my side, purring and pushing his nose into my hand or my face to let me know that he was concerned. Now, he was coming to me for that same comfort and I was only glad that I was able to provide it for him.

If forced to examine the details of my own life, I will admit that I am a selfish person. I have lived my life the way I want to live it, within reason of course (I haven't actually murdered all the people who work for the phone company, which I have often been tempted to do, so I understand that my selfishness and self-absorption have limits). I have defied several conventions and tried to follow my own course as much as possible. I've had a strange career because I opted to do several things instead of focusing on just one. As a result, I've made a lot less money than I could have, but money has never been a motivating factor for me. My own satisfaction is much more of a guide. On a personal level, I have an excellent and long-lasting relationship but have never gotten married (and just to anticipate more letter writers, no, we still don't even live together—I'm too selfish and, luckily, she's got certain saintlike qualities that allow for it). Marriage is another convention and ritual I don't believe in. No one is going to tell me, by saying a few words, giving me a piece of paper and having me exchange rings, that I now have something permanent and valuable. *I'll* decide what's permanent and valuable, that's my attitude. I've never had kids. Always thought I'd want 'em eventually but guess what—I'm in my late forties and "eventually" still isn't here. I've turned down big jobs and chosen most of my relationships with people purely on the basis of friendship rather than usefulness or value to me. And when you add it all up, I think it's fair to say that I'm one of the few people who truly likes the life he's leading, *really* likes it and has few regrets. A very big part of that is because I've been able to live selfishly.

But treating Norton, once he got cancer, taught me the joys of living unselfishly. No, "taught" isn't exactly the right word. It's not something that can *be* taught. It's something that must be experienced. And what I experienced was the feeling—and the ensuing knowledge—that there was practically nothing I wouldn't do for my cat if it allowed me to give him just a little bit of the same pleasure he'd given me for most of my adult life.

As that great philosopher Søren Kierkegaard once said: "Go know."

Okay, that's kind of a paraphrase.

Anyway . . .

I took care of Norton as best I could and he did just fine. He was happy, he seemed healthy, he did stuff, he was in no pain. The two-month deadline given to me by the oncologist came and went. So did the nine-month deadline. A full year passed since the cancer had struck him and then *another* six months passed. Outwardly, Norton showed no signs of really weakening or being in any way un-Norton-like. Except for the still too prevalent throwing up and the occasional accident away from the litter box, he was the same old Scottish Fold wunderkind.

For almost two years.

He had that will to live, I guess.

Then I noticed he was losing weight again

And he seemed a little wobbly when jumping from bed to floor. Then just walking around . . .

And those damn blood tests kept getting faxed to me

and too many counts were suddenly either too low or too high.

So I went back to Dr. Dianne DeLorenzo to see what was what.

And what it was was the beginning of the end.

CHAPTER 10

THE CAT
WHO WENT BACK
ON THE ROAD

T he cancer was spreading.

That was the word from Dianne DeLorenzo and this time I accepted it. I could see it. For the first time since I'd first met my little cat, when he was six weeks old and fresh off a plane from Los Angeles, he looked frail.

The treatments continued, of course, and I took as perfect care of him as always. One of the bonuses, as far as Norton was concerned, was that I basically said, "Fuck it," and decided he could now eat whatever he wanted. I wasn't going back to the horrendous canned cat food—that would have been like saying to a dying man, "Okay, you get to eat nothing but McDonald's the rest of your life"—but I knew that what he particularly liked was shrimp. He liked it much more than chicken, much much more than hamburger meat or even steak. It wasn't the absolutely best thing for him but my cat loved shrimp so at this stage of his life shrimp is what he got. Twice a day if he so desired, although I tried to vary it so he wouldn't get sick of it (although he *never* seemed to get sick of it). I'll even confess that I usually bought this shrimp at the best seafood markets, at places like Balducci's, so it was fresh and perfect. Once, though, I was at my neighborhood supermarket and I was pressed for time, so I bought a packet of shrimp from their fish section. It was perfectly fine, it just wasn't, you know, the best. But as I was heading to the checkout line, an elderly woman, and clearly a woman who lived on a budget, stopped me and told me that the shrimp I was buying looked delicious. Without thinking, I said that it was for my cat. She said, "You must be very well off. I buy that twice a year for myself—as a treat." Horrified at my thoughtless blunder, I tried to stammer my way out of it and said, "Well, I like my cat quite a lot." And she got a wistful, faraway look in her eyes and said, "I'd like to *be* your cat." I told her that a lot of people felt the same way, and I asked if she'd mind if I bought her a little present. She said she wouldn't mind one bit, so I bought and gave her another couple of pounds of shrimp. She was very pleased.

In addition to his daily, and often twice-daily, pleasure when munching on his *crevettes*, Norton still had some major periods of remission where he felt absolutely fine. A couple of these remissions came after Marty prescribed Epogin, which brings the red blood cell count back up and stops the anemia. The more amazing remission came when Marty sent me something called Poly-MVA. Marty had recently seen it work wonders, and even Dianne's partner, another superb doctor named Ann Wayne Lucas, had witnessed something remarkable in a cat who'd taken it. Dr. Lucas had seen a tumor—a lymph cancer on this cat's nose, one that everyone thought was days away from killing the cat—not just shrink but flat out disappear.

So I administered a few doses of Poly-MVA, as instructed (for this one I had to use a hypodermic needle) and sure enough certain things improved and Norton was a lot happier, but by this time it was a stopgap treatment and even I had to admit it. I had to accept, once and for all, that sooner rather than later, I was going to be catless.

I cried a little in Dianne's office as we discussed all this (All right, all right, get off my back—I cried *a lot*! But I'm trying to remain somewhat manly here). She didn't know exactly how long Norton would live. It could be several months still, she said. But it could be weeks. Once this wretched disease starts to spread, it can spread quickly. And it can wreak havoc.

She also brought up something that I had never even considered. No, that's not right. It was something that I had not ever let myself consider. She started to explain to me that, at some point—not *now*, she immediately stressed when she saw the look on my face—but when and if it was necessary, I'd have to make a decision about putting him to sleep. I nodded, as if this was something I could absolutely deal with like a mature adult, then I started to ask a question and burst out sobbing. This went on for a few seconds until I wiped my tears, composed myself, decided I was okay, and started to ask the question all over again. I got maybe the first word out of my mouth, burst back into tears, and had to sit there in her office, chest heaving, feeling like an idiot. Luckily, Dianne had experienced this before—many times before—and she could not only anticipate my questions and finish my sentences for me, she could give me compassionate answers. This was a good thing because, try as I might, I could not speak.

"What about . . . when . . . when . . ." I'd say and then the crying would start again.

"What about when it's time," Dr. DeLorenzo would prompt me and I'd manage to nod. "First of all," she said, "you have a great understanding of your cat and you'll *understand* when it's time. You'll know. I promise you. And you shouldn't do it until you know it's right."

Then I said something like, "And . . . (sob) . . . when it is . . . (sniffle) . . . right . . . (choked back sob) . . . what do . . . ? . . . (torrential tears) . . ."

Dr. DeLorenzo: You can bring him in here.

Me: Will . . . ? . . . (major crying jag)

Dr. DeLorenzo: Yes. I'll do it. You can be with him and even hold him if you want.

Me: (Not even close to getting a real word out, just body-wracking sobs.)

In between my bouts of hysteria, Dianne managed to explain that if I wanted Norton to die at home, there were some doctors who'd come to the apartment to perform the service. But I said no, I wanted her to do it. Well, I didn't actually say it. I gasped and snorted and got a few syllables out that sounded something vaguely like it. I then tried once again to ask a practical question. I wanted to know about cremation. I tried two or three times on this one but never actually got past the hard *c* sound without having to go for the Kleenex. Dianne understood, once again, and told me that she could and would handle the whole thing. It was not something I had to worry about.

Then she said something wonderful, both sad and sweet and totally accurate.

"The only thing wrong with our pets," Dianne DeLorenzo told me, "is that they don't live as long as we do."

I was giving Norton his IV drip every day now and those minutes we spent all alone were minutes I knew we both valued. We were connected as two living creatures rarely are. And because I was so aware of that connection, I had an idea.

I kept it to myself for a little while. Let it percolate to see if it would linger or disappear. It lingered. Particularly when we went out to Sag Harbor in mid-April. Over that weekend, the idea took form—and then took over my thoughts completely.

While in Sag Harbor, Norton was as active as he'd been in weeks and weeks. He insisted on jumping on and off the bed, even though he really couldn't jump very well. At the end of each leap, he'd mostly sprawl and slide along the bedroom floor's wooden planks. I showed him how he could use the antique trunk at the foot of the bed as a mid-way stopping point—both on the way up and on the way down—but he didn't like that idea. He finally used it to get up on the bed but he refused to acknowledge its existence when he'd hop down. I think he felt it wasn't dignified. A cat was supposed to be able to get down on his own from a bed, so that's what he was determined to do. For these few days, he absolutely refused to give in to the fact that his body was playing such awful tricks on him. When we'd leave him downstairs, even for a few minutes, he'd somehow go up the stairs to join us (this was the first time he had trouble climbing; each step was difficult for him, because it was steep, but that didn't stop him). He ate a ton, more than he had in a long time. All weekend he meowed for food and whenever I'd put some in his bowl, he'd gobble it down.

I have this theory about aging. I think that as people get older, they become more and more like their real selves. If you're cranky as a young person, the older you get the more crotchety you'll be. If you're fearful, old age brings terror. If you're rigid, when you hit a certain time of life you'll be as unbendable as a flagpole. If you're a loner, there will come a time when all you're going to want is to become a hermit. Age brings out one's quirks and allows them to flourish and, I guess, it brings down defenses and restraints so there's no choice but to *let* them flourish. My cat was a perfect example. As Norton aged and got closer to death, he got sweeter. Gentler. And even more courageous. It was quite something to see.

Over the past few weeks, I had finally told people that Norton was sick. It was now obvious, so I didn't think there was any more reason for secrecy. Once the word was out, calls started coming in. I was actually a little stunned. People were calling to see how I was holding up, sure, but really they were concerned for Norton and wanted to show that concern. He was one of *them*—and they wanted to acknowledge that. Susan Burden (she's the one we visited the day Norton saw President Clinton) told me that she called her mother down in Florida to tell her that Norton had cancer and she said her mother burst into tears. Nancy Alderman called to check up on the little guy. After I filled her in, she put her son Charlie on the phone. We chatted and hung up. Nancy called me back a few moments later because she said she'd asked Charlie if he'd asked me about Norton. Charlie—in a hushed tone—said, "Oh no, I didn't *mention* Norton." There was something very sweet about a nine-year-old boy trying to protect me from the pain he knew I was experiencing.

Several writers I worked with called me during this period to see how my guy was doing. My close friend Micheline called every day. Norm Stiles, who now had his own amazingly adorable Scottish Fold named Gozzie, called practically hourly. I had talked to my old friend Roman Polanski, who had shared many experiences with Norton in Paris. Roman was pained to hear about my cat's decline and he called that weekend in Sag Harbor to check up on him. Almost everyone I knew who also knew Norton called to check up on him that weekend. It was over-whelming.

I took him in to see Drs. Turetsky and Pepper, for the first time in months; they were surprised at Norton's fragility. Pepper examined him very, very gently. When I told him that Norton was having trouble going to the bath-room, that it seemed to really pain him each time he got in the litter box, the vet gave him an enema (this was the only thing I felt I just couldn't bring myself to do, although I think we all know by now that if I had to, I would have). Dr. Pepper also weighed Norton. He was down to five pounds (from his normal nine). "He's an amazing little cat," Turetsky said when I was leaving and I knew that was his way of paying respect and saying his farewell to his long-time patient. Which is really why I had brought him there.

I waited until we got back to the city before I finally discussed my big idea with Janis. I expected her to say that I was crazy or, at the very least, a sentimental fool. Instead, she smiled and nodded and told me that she thought it was an excellent idea. When I tried to argue myself out of my own plan, she told me to stop thinking so much and just get on with it. I needed closure, she said. I needed something special that would help me get over what was sure to be a devastating loss. She said that my idea was indeed special. And that it felt right. And then she said what I really wanted to hear: that Norton would love it.

So I went to see Dr. DeLorenzo and told her what I wanted to do. She thought it was a little odd but by now she was used to odd when it came to me and Norton, so she gave me the thumbs-up. She said that I should be prepared for the fact that Norton could fade at any time—and fade quickly—but for the moment he looked to be able to handle the adventure I was proposing. Then she asked the key question: Was *I* able to handle the adventure I was proposing?

I told her I wasn't sure. But I was going to give it a shot.

My idea was a simple one: Norton and I had spent much of our lives together traveling. We'd been all over Europe. We'd flown around most of America. We'd spent a huge portion of our existence together in hotels and motels and fantasy houses in medieval villages, in cars and planes and buses and boats. We'd dined out together in exotic places, sharing meals and unique experiences. We'd gone to major sporting events and nightclubs and offices and sales conferences and we'd met interesting, weird, brilliant, sometimes crazy people. Quite simply, the most fun both of us had had over the past sixteen-plus years was when we were on the road doing what we both liked the best: experiencing new things, taking chances and doing our best to keep life from ever getting dull and predictable.

So here's what I wanted to do: I wanted to go back on the road with Norton.

I wanted to share some of his final moments on earth the way we'd shared so many of the vital moments that had defined both of our lives. Together. Just the two of us. I wanted to do what so many people never got a chance to do.

I wanted one final trip with my cat so I could say goodbye.

I moved quickly, decided that the way to go was to see some new sights, have a few new adventures, but mostly return to some of Norton's favorite places.

I planned this so thoroughly, taking care of every little detail, making sure that I thought of absolutely everything and every possible contingency, that I felt a little bit like I was going off on my honeymoon.

"I think I might have crossed the line and become a total lunatic," I said to Janis the morning we were leaving.

"You *think?*" she said. And as I winced, she gave Norton a gentle and tender pat, gave me a not-so-gentle but equally tender kiss, and told us, "Just go. Just go and the two of you have a very, very good time."

I had packed everything that might be needed: several

litter boxes (one for the floor of the front seat, one for the back, so he would never be more than a step away) several bags of litter, towels (in case Norton didn't make the litter boxes, either in the car or in the places we were staying), drip bags, needles, medicine, bottled water, food (I even brought some fresh-cooked shrimp in a small insulated Styrofoam box, packed in ice, in case I couldn't find something that Norton liked along the way). I had special travel bowls for food and water so Norton could have whatever he wanted while we drove. And I took a whole bunch of catnip (I figured it was like medicinal marijuana. There's nothing my cat liked better, in the whole world, than a little taste of catnip, so I figured why not keep him rolling in the stuff). My little red car looked like a MASH unit by the time it was full.

When I was certain there was absolutely nothing left to take that he could possibly need, I put him in his shoulder bag—he weighed so little now and the impact of that hit me so hard as we were walking to the car that carrying him on my shoulder nearly brought tears to my eyes—and we were off.

I knew I'd made the right decision almost as soon as the drive began.

I have a small, 1989 BMW convertible. My father bought it soon before he died and he loved this car. My mother loved it just as much but when she moved to New York she didn't need or want it anymore. So I was allowed to buy it from her cheap (*very* cheap: one dollar). And I was as crazy about this automobile as both my parents were. But not as crazy as Norton was.

You see, Norton had discovered something about the car the very first winter that I had it. He and I were driving together from Sag Harbor back to the city. Norton was sitting in the passenger seat and when I glanced over at him I thought he seemed particularly happy and content. He was purring away as only the happiest of cats could. At first I was quite touched, thinking he was just pleased to be with me, and so near (Janis wasn't making this drive, so Norton didn't have to stay in the back). But that wasn't it at all. What I realized was that the car had switches in between the two seats: black switches that activated individual seat warmers. Norton was so happy that particular winter two-hour drive not because he was next to me but because he'd accidentally hit the switch and his seat was toasty warm. And so was he.

At least I'd *thought* it was accidental.

Naturally, I had once again underestimated my pal.

Because from then on, every time Norton was in the car and allowed to sit by himself in the front seat, he'd casually reach over, flick the seat warming switch, curl up in a ball and settle in for a perfect ride.

As we were pulling out of the city on our final voyage, I wondered if he was too feeble to bother or if he'd go for the heat.

The answer, of course, was yes, heat all the way. Cancer be damned, he was going to be as comfortable as he could be. Before we'd even gotten a full block away, his paw was stretching in my direction, the button was pressed, and Norton was purring away.

He purred all the way to Washington, D.C., which I'd decided was going to be our first stop. I had not spent much time there and neither had Norton, but it seemed like a fitting place to begin. We checked into the Madison Hotel—nice, not far from the White House, and reasonably cat-friendly. I wasn't sure if he'd be up to any sight-seeing but once we were settled and he'd had a little shrimp, he seemed quite game. So we headed out and Norton saw the Lincoln Memorial for the first time, and the Vietnam War Memorial. We also sat for a bit in the park across from the White House but there was no dog run, so for Norton it was not nearly as interesting as what he was used to. After a while I decided he'd had enough excitement, so we headed back to the Madison.

Because we'd done so much touring, I thought it would be better if we shared a room service meal instead of dining out. Norton was grateful to get his second IV drip of the day—I'd gone to twice a day for the past couple of weeks; he always seemed to feel so much better after-ward—then eat a little grilled chicken and get to bed.

The next morning, we were headed for Pennsylvania, but our first stop was Valley Forge. We got out of the car at the very spot where George Washington crossed the Delaware. I felt like there should be some spiritual or, at the very least, symbolic connection. Something that tied it all together—the beginning and the end, the long ago adven-ture that created something big and great and the modern adventure that was ending something small and great. But I couldn't find anything and neither, I'm sure, could Norton. We just weren't big on symbols. Nonetheless, it was an impressive spot, awe inspiring as only history can be. So we soaked in the atmosphere, got back in the car, and then we drove back to one of Norton's favorite bed-and-breakfasts, Sweetwater Farm.

For those of you who haven't been paying attention, Sweetwater was the site of my aunt Belle's encounter with the goat on one of our Spring Trips. It was a beautiful and extraordinary place. The main house was an old stone building, going back to the 1700s. There were several out-buildings that had been converted into individual rooms or suites, some stone, some wood. There were many acres of lush land, a swimming pool, and near the pool was a lovely mesh tree swing. By the swing, placed under a large oak tree, were wooden chairs and a wooden love seat.

Cherry trees were scattered around the property and, in the few years since we'd been there with our Spring Group, they'd added more horses, and the fenced-in corrals had been greatly improved.

I checked in with Rick and Grace, the husband and wife innkeepers, who were happy to see me and, as always, happier to see Norton. I could see, however, that they were startled at his appearance. Even just poking his head out of the shoulder bag to say hello, they could tell that he wasn't well. Rick gave him a friendly, soft pat on the head and looked at me sadly. I nodded. I had decided that nodding was, in general, my best course of action, because it was difficult to cry if you nodded hard enough.

We got the same room we'd been in when we first stayed there: a suite in one of the small wooden buildings, the Gardener's Cottage, on the property. There was a porch, a sitting room, a bedroom and a bathroom. And I immediately went about setting it up for Norton's comfort. So he didn't have to move if he didn't want to, I put food and water bowls down in both the sitting room and bedroom, did the same with the litter boxes, and rigged the drip bag up in the bathroom. Then I took him outside and we sat in the shade of the oak tree, on the wooden love seat, for most of the afternoon. I did what were to become my two favorite activities on this trip—I read and I cried.

I guess I should warn you that you're going to have to get used to the fact that you're going to hear a lot about me crying for a while, because I don't think I made it through one whole sentence on this trip without having to stop and let a few tears escape. Sitting on the bench, doing both of those things, sometimes one, sometimes the other, sometimes both at once, Norton mostly sat with me, but he also did a little wandering in the high grass. He didn't wander too far, however. Walking was not his best thing by this time. He reminded me a little bit of Terry Malloy, the Brando character, after he'd been beaten up at the end of *On the Waterfront*, walking into the warehouse so he could break the evil union. Norton was unsteady, he lurched and was usually at a tilt—but, like Brando, he never fell. That strong will, you know. It was still working full blast.

From time to time during the day, when he wasn't either keeping me company or exploring, he'd hop off the bench, do his version of walking, find the perfect sunny spot, settle in and doze. When I was neither reading nor crying, I'd watch him. He looked handsome there in the grass. And because he'd gotten so small, to me he looked young and healthy—like a kitten again. It was a nice thing to see: Norton in the grass, butterflies fluttering, birds chirping everywhere. It was as serene a setting as could be imagined. And it was peaceful. Norton wasn't sick. Not now, not outwardly. He wasn't throwing up. He wasn't in pain. He was just quiet, sitting there in the sun.

He was just fading.

Occasionally, he would meow. A sweet mew, not at all cranky. Norton had a distinctive happy meow—it was brisk, trilling, a "brrrrr-brrrr-brrrr" sound, like a putt-putt motor boat with a tiny bit of a Scottish accent—and this was definitely his happy sound. I think those mews were letting me know I'd done the right thing.

We stayed at Sweetwater Farm for a couple of days. At night, we'd go back to the common room in the main house. I shot pool on the red felt table until the early morning hours while Norton sat in the comfortable wing chair, on top of a thick blanket with a picture of a polo player on it, and watched. But, almost hour by hour, all day and all night, I could see him fade just a little bit more.

Despite the twice daily drips he was getting, Norton wasn't going to the bathroom very often now. I'd had so much medical training by this time, I knew what that meant. His whole system was failing. He was not able to expunge the disease—diseases, really—that had overtaken his body. He had lost so much muscle, that's why he was having trouble walking and jumping and now even performing the normal bodily functions. Even the small intestines need muscle to function—and the cancer had eaten most of Norton's muscle away.

It was all happening very quickly. Two or three weeks earlier, my cat did not look sick and did not act sick. Now the disease was in overdrive. It was getting nearer and nearer to the end. I remembered something that Marty Goldstein had told me when I had called him to say that things were getting worse. He compared Norton to the Ukrainian peasants who lived to be a hundred and thirty. They die quickly, he said. We're used to stretching death out—we die for about one-third of our lives. Those peasants are healthy, then, boom, they're gone. That's the way it should be, Marty said. Live a good life, stay healthy as long as possible, then die. That's what was happening to

Norton, he said, and I should be grateful that he was getting to go out this way.

I was. Really. I remembered that a few months before,
I was with my mother when she'd called her two oldest
friends. It was one of the worst conversations I'd ever
heard. First the husband answered—this is someone my
mother had known for fifty years. I heard my mom say,
"Henry, it's Judy." Then she said it again: "*Judy.*" Then she
had to say, "Judy *Gethers*," and then I saw this horrified
look on my mother's face as she realized he didn't have a
clue who she was. She tried to explain but the more she did
the worse it got. She finally asked him to put Vera, his wife,
on the phone, but when he complied, my mother started to
cry—I guess you can tell we're related—and couldn't talk
to her. I had to get on the phone and make a few excuses
before hanging up. It was just a terrible thing to be privy
to. It was something that shouldn't happen to anyone, that
ebbing of one's faculties, that state of living but not really
living. So yes, I was glad that wasn't happening to my cat.
But it didn't make what *was* happening any easier.

I thought about heading home with him after our stay
at Sweetwater, but as Dianne DeLorenzo had said, I understood my cat. I had a very strong sense of what was right
or wrong and I decided he was enjoying this. I truly think
he understood the whole concept of closure and that he
wanted to play this through to the end as much as I did.

So we headed off in our mobile medical unit, a.k.a.
The Red Beamer, to go to Charlottesville, Virginia.

This was another town that Norton had loved and
when the car cruised in, I drove slowly through the city's
downtown streets as Norton sat up, craned his neck, and

looked out the window at the sights. We didn't stop for lunch, though. I wanted to get Norton all set up at the hotel, so we went straight to one of the great inns in the country, the Clifton.

It was a thrilling place, for both of us. The manor house was built in 1799 by Thomas Randolph, a governor of the state and the husband of Thomas Jefferson's daughter Martha. There were all sorts of legends about the house concerning the Civil War years, when it was owned by John Singleton Mosby, the "Grey Ghost of the Confederacy," who supposedly used secret hiding places in the mansion to store supplies and provisions, aiding those Johnny Rebs in their fight against the Yankees.

We were put up in a suite which was, years before, part of the original stable on the property. Even by Norton's high standards for comfort, the place was a gem. It was separate from the main house, providing plenty of privacy, and it overlooked the gorgeous gardens as well as Lake Leanna, the property's private lake. The bedroom had a queen-size bed and beautiful wooden floor and there was a sitting room with a rocking chair and a comfortable window seat. And there was my cat's favorite thing in the whole world: a fireplace.

I put Norton in his bag and took him over to the main house so he could check things out (I'm sure you've picked up by this late point that I didn't want my cat to miss out on anything). The people at the hotel went absolutely wild over him. Everyone came out to meet him. The manager had read the two books about him—a friend of his had given them to him long before I'd thought of bringing Norton down there. The executive chef, Rachel, provided a shrimp wrapped in bacon which, needless to say, my pal gobbled down immediately. Linda, the woman at the desk, told me that she raised dogs but had recently become a cat fanatic—and now had five of them. She sensed that Norton was sick—possibly I gave it away when she asked me how old he was and my eyes welled up with tears, I got short of breath and I had to sit down. It was a pretty good hint. He was sitting up in his bag, his upper body out in the open, and she stroked him gently and told him how beautiful he was. Then she said that even if his body was going to die, his spirit would live on. I responded that I wasn't too sure about people's spirits—but I thought that Norton's spirit at least had a decent chance. She immediately decided I was a heathen—I recognize the look by now—but she clearly didn't hold it against my cat because she kept stroking him and talking to him and he was about as happy as he could be.

That night he was invited to dine in the dining room, breaking *all* their hard and fast rules, but I could tell he was cranky and tired, so I took him back to our room. I brought with us some more of the chef's shrimp in bacon, so I knew Norton wouldn't be unhappy dining alone.

I guess I needed a break—it was a little bit like traveling with one's invalid grandfather—because dining alone, I was absolutely ravenous and I felt calmer than I'd felt in a long time. I ate well (the Clifton's restaurant is superb; the meal was highlighted by local fresh vegetables and edible local flowers, including a champagne pansy sauce—no cracks, please—that was poured over the grapefruit sorbet dessert) and drank a bottle of Virginia red wine. I wanted to drink about seven bottles, but I settled for draining every last drop of the one.

By dessert time, though, I couldn't stand it—so I went

and got Norton and brought him back for the final course. He was unobtrusive sitting in the chair opposite me. He meowed once or twice, I gave him a couple of teaspoons of the champagne pansy sauce, which he quite liked, and then we strolled back to the room, both of us content.

The only thing that worried me at the Clifton was the bed. It was beautiful and large—but it was also dangerously high with Norton being so fragile. I didn't want to risk his jumping off and hurting himself but, selfishly, I wanted him with me. So for that night, I slept on my back, cradling him in my arms. Three or four times during the night, he moved, wanting to get down. So I carried him to his food or water or litter box. He did what he wanted to do, then I'd put him back in my arms, get back into bed and go back to sleep—until the next time he wanted down. We both seemed quite happy with the arrangement.

The next day, Norton was doing well so we did a little touring. I took him to Monticello, which I genuinely think is the one place every person in America must visit. What you come away feeling, after a tour of Jefferson's home, is not just a sense of pride, awe and historical perspective. What you mostly leave with is a sense of total and absolute inadequacy.

In case you ever are feeling smug or self-satisfied, consider this: Thomas Jefferson had engraved on his tombstone the three accomplishments of which he was most proud. Being president of the United States wasn't one of them! For the record, he picked writing the Constitution of the United States, writing the Religious Freedom Act of the state of Virginia and founding the University of Virginia. I know that if *I* were ever president of the United States, I'd

pretty much *have* to put that as one of my three top accomplishments (And you'll have to trust me here: you
don't want to know what the other two are. The only hint
I'll give is that one of them involves a former Miss
Bermuda).

When you go through Monticello, you find out that
Thomas Jefferson brought the first roses to America. He
was our country's first and greatest gardener. He grew the
first grapes and was America's first vintner. He brought
French food to us. He built the first clock that not only
kept time but kept track of the days for up to a week. In his
study upstairs, he had (because he invented it) the first
copying machine. I swear! There was this amazing contraption that he concocted because he knew he was
Thomas Jefferson and that people would want records of
everything he did. The way this thing worked is that
whenever he wrote something, the machine was attached
to his arm, a pen was attached to the machine and the
whole thing moved along with him in a mirror image,
making a duplicate copy of what he was writing. So you
walk out of there thinking that Jefferson invented food,
wine, government, freedom, the Xerox machine, America
and just about everything else you've ever heard of. Just
walking to the parking lot with Norton, I was certain that
not only had Jefferson invented parking lots, he probably
invented the very air we were breathing!

After Monticello, Norton still seemed pretty active, so
we went off to the University of Virginia and took a quick
tour. We sat on the campus for a little while which, even
with no dog run, obviously impressed Norton, and then
we hit the almost indescribable Rotunda, the library which

Jefferson designed (I'm sure he was not only our first architect, he probably invented the whole idea of books! You know, he's starting to steam me!).

After this academic tour, it was time to return to the Clifton. We relaxed the rest of the afternoon while I got in my daily quotient of reading and weeping, then we had dinner together in the dining room. Norton was exhausted and dozed through almost the entire meal. He perked up for another teaspoon of the champagne sauce, and even a little bit of the sorbet, but other than that, he slept while I guzzled more Virginia pinot noir.

The next morning, I decided our road trip was over. During the night, I sensed that Norton had taken a turn for the worse. He was logy and suddenly, for the first time, his legs were buckling when he walked. Several times in the middle of the night, I carried him to his food and water dishes as well as to the litter box. I'd done that before because I knew it was easier for him. But now, for the first time, I did it because I didn't think he could walk there himself.

In the car, heading north, I had a lot of time to reflect. I thought about a poem by Gerard Manley Hopkins called "Margaret, Are You Grieving?" I am hardly a poetry expert. Most of the poems and poets I know I read in college. Okay, *all* of the poems and poets I know I read in college, except for the contemporary classics that begin with things like, "There was a young man from Nantucket." Actually, that's not totally true. When Janis and I were first dating, I did read Yeats and Donne and William Carlos Williams aloud to her, but that was so she'd think I was sensitive and would have sex with me, so I'm not positive that really counts. But driving along, the Hopkins poem kept entering my head. It's a brilliant piece of writing, basically about the fact that when we grieve for those who die, what we're really doing is grieving for ourselves. We're really mourning our *own* mortality. Despite what some people might think, I'm not a total nut. I knew—and know—that Norton was a cat, that he wasn't a child or a member of my family. But having perspective doesn't necessarily alleviate the sadness one feels. I tried to think what it was that made me love my cat so much, what it was that was forcing such grief upon me. When my father died, I did exactly what the Hopkins poem said we all do. I knew I was grieving for myself—at what I had lost, at what I would miss by not having my father around, at the wound which would remain with me forever as a result of losing him. With Norton it was different. Yes, of course I was grieving for myself. I was going to miss this little creature who had somehow, over the years, meowed his way into my heart to become my very best friend and my treasured companion. Norton loved me, had since the day we met, and I loved him in return. That love was real and powerful and valuable. So in that sense, I was grieving for what I was losing. We do not—me or anyone else—have such an abundance of love in our lives that we can cavalierly gloss over its disappearance, when it does indeed disappear. But I knew this was more than that.

I believe I was genuinely grieving over my cat himself.

The only way I can possibly explain it is that people are flawed. Even the best people. And even those we deeply love evoke mixed and complicated emotions because along with that love there is always some amount of pain or frustration or compromise, there is always some other complexity in relationships between humans. Norton was *not* flawed. He was, in fact, perfect. He could *be* perfect because he was a simpler creature than most human beings. He gave without demanding anything (other than cat treats and the occasional stomach scratch). He comforted without complaint. He provided companionship and compassion and as I realized all this, I decided my grief was not just valid, it was important, because Norton's death was not going to just be a loss for me, it was going to be a loss for everyone. There is not so much of that perfection thing going around that we can afford to lose it without grieving.

While I drove, and thought these morbid thoughts, Norton sat in his warmed-up seat, although this time I flicked the switch for him since he did not have the strength to do it himself. I talked to him the entire way back to New York. Told him how wonderful he was, told him how much I was going to miss him. He'd meow grumpily—not in pain but in a kind of anger and annoyance. It was as if he were saying, "Why can't I jump up and sit on your shoulder like I used to?" I could tell he was frustrated. He didn't understand what was happening to him. Or why he couldn't jump or walk or even pee the way he should. He was also embarrassed, I think, at his physical condition, and about the fact that I had to see him like this. I kept one hand on him most of the time I drove. And I told him that he shouldn't be angry or embarrassed. That he was as perfect as a thing could be.

I could see how really weak he was now. Occasionally he would force himself up on his haunches so he could look out the window—always one of his favorite activities. But mostly he lay still. Sometimes when he meowed, I could tell he was thirsty. But he didn't have the energy to get to his bowl of water. I kept a bottle of water next to me,

so periodically I'd wet my fingers and let him lick the water off. It made me grin because I always loved the feel of
his rough tongue on me. Cats don't smile, so I couldn't be
positive, but I was pretty sure he enjoyed it, too—the water and the familiar touch and taste of my skin.

By the time we'd gotten halfway to the city, I was a
mournful shell of a human being. We actually passed two
funeral processions along the way. I'm not kidding. Each
time we saw one, I totally lost control. As the second one
passed, I tried calling Janis on my cell phone but all I could
do was sob. Somehow, she knew it was me (I wonder
how?!) and she just said, "It's okay, you don't have to talk.
Just call me when you can."

To totally wallow in my melancholy, I played Loudon
Wainwright CDs the whole way. He is just about my favorite singer-musician and almost every one of his songs
was about someone leaving or growing old or going away
or dying. It must have been a strange sight to anyone who
happened to glance into my car. For quite a few hours, all
they would have seen was a man driving, talking to his cat,
and blubbering like a madman.

Back in New York, back in our Washington Square apartment, I did everything I could to make Norton as comfortable as possible. It didn't take long before walking was
an impossible feat for him. Soon, almost everything else
was just as impossible. His breathing was heavy and forced,
his meowing was weak. His appetite was nonexistent. Even
his favorite, shrimp, was left untouched in his bowl.

On Friday, May 7, I went to give him his IV drip but

he was so skinny I couldn't find any extra flesh in which to put the needle. Holding him on my lap, I could feel that his skin was now completely dry. It was crinkly, almost like a snake skin, or like Saran Wrap when you touch it. I petted him as gently as I could, but it felt as if under the fur his skin would slide right off his body. When he looked at me sadly, I knew he didn't even want his drip. So I didn't bother. I knew what he wanted. I held him on my lap for quite a while, didn't say anything for a change, just touching him and sometimes kissing him, and made the hardest decision I've ever made in my life.

When Janis came over after work, I told her that I'd tried three times to call the receptionist at Dianne De-Lorenzo's office to make an appointment for the next morning to put Norton to sleep. I also told her that each time I'd called, as soon as the receptionist answered the phone, I had burst into tears and been unable to speak. She asked me if I was sure this was the right thing and the right time and I remembered what Dianne had told me: I'd know. She was absolutely right. I did know. There was no doubt. So I nodded—that nodding trick was still work-ing—and Janis called the Washington Square Animal Hospital, spoke to the receptionist, and made the appoint-ment for nine-thirty the next morning.

That night, I asked Janis if she'd mind not staying at my apartment. I wanted Norton to be as comfortable as possi-ble and I wanted him to sleep with me. I wanted to be next to him for one final time and because his set-up was so elaborate—I had him in my bed, with towels all around him, food and water right next to him—I didn't think there'd be room for all three of us. Janis ain't no dummy—she knew what I really wanted was just to be alone with my cat on his final night on earth—so she kissed us both and went to her own place around nine o'clock at night.

By ten, my cat and I were both in bed. I was exhausted (You know what? Crying all the time is *very* tiring). I had Norton tucked in under the covers, his head on the pillow, the way he liked best to sleep. I was next to him, turned on my side so I could both watch him and touch him whenever I wanted to.

I slept, but not at all soundly. Periodically, I'd get up and wet my fingers with water and then let him lick the tips. His breathing was raspy and heavy.

At one-thirty in the morning, I awoke with a start. I could hear him coughing. Not loudly, more of a quiet choking noise, as if he was clearing his throat. I put my hand on his head, softly and as gently as I was able. His breathing was very slow now. Regular but almost imperceptibly soft. I took him out of the covers, picked him up and cradled him in my arms. As I did, he began purring. We sat that way for about half an hour while I stroked him and kissed him and told him how much I loved him and how much I was going to miss him.

And then Norton showed me how much he loved me, too.

Of every single thing that had happened and that I knew was going to happen, the one thing I was dreading the most was putting him to sleep. I knew I could do it, knew I would even be strong enough to be there in the room, but the idea of it was just as awful as anything I'd ever envisioned. I didn't want my cat to go that way. I didn't want to see it and I didn't want to have to think about it the rest of my life.

So Norton spared me that.

He had done many amazing things during his life, from learning to unlock our bedroom door to keeping me company by walking miles along a crowded beach to operating his own automobile seat warmer. But now he did the most amazing thing he'd ever done.

At two o'clock in the morning, on May 8, 1999, Norton purred right up until he closed his eyes, took one last shallow breath, and died in my arms.

CHAPTER 11

THE CAT WHO'LL
LIVE FOREVER

The aftermath of death is an interesting and strange thing.

The immediate sensation was one of surprising calm and relief.

The moment Norton died my tears stopped.

It's not that I wasn't overcome with loss, it's simply that death itself was so much more peaceful for him than the last two or three days of his life. I was instantly overcome with the realization that he was gone and that all the good things I loved about him were now part of my memory rather than the present. That is always a jarring emotional adjustment, because we all place so much more value on the here and now than we do on memory—but the fact is that he was no longer in pain and, about that, I was glad.

I held him for a fairly long time, maybe fifteen minutes or so, until I was absolutely sure he was dead. I'd never been in this situation before, so while I was as certain as I could be that his breathing had stopped, I didn't want to be mourning him and suddenly have him meow and startle me to my own death. So I sat there and stroked him and finally accepted the fact that yes, he was gone. I remembered what the woman from the hospice had told me about my dad when he was dying, so I kept my hand on his chest, was strangely comforted by the contact and the intimacy. After a while, I kissed him on top of the head, and decided that was my final physical goodbye.

The trauma was over, the crying had ended, and now reality was setting in. I sat there, trying to decide what to do—sleep was out of the question—and decided that it was okay to call Janis, even if it was now two-thirty in the morning. When the phone rang, she knew who it was and why I was calling. I told her that Norton had died, she asked if I wanted her to come over and I said no, that I was okay, really, and this time I was telling the truth.

But when I hung up, I realized that I did have a new problem to deal with.

I've explained that "squeamish" might as well be my middle name, so I was not able to simply shrug off the slightly ghoulish situation facing me. That situation was that, with all the calm and peace and intimacy surrounding me, there was no getting around the fact that I had a non-living cat in my bed.

I called Janis back and said, "What the *hell* am I supposed to do now?"

What I finally did was call Dr. DeLorenzo's office and the night operator gave me a number for Manhattan's twenty-four-hour animal hospital. I called them, told them of my situation, and the woman there asked if I had a bag.

"What kind of bag?" I asked.

"A bag that your cat'll fit into," she said, not as sensitively as she might have.

I said that I probably did and she explained that I should put him in the bag, cover him up with a blanket, and bring him to my regular vet in the morning. I said, "That's it?" and she answered, "Well, what else did you have in mind?" I decided I wouldn't utter exactly what I had in mind for her, simply said, "Okay," hung up and looked over at Norton. The strangest thing about what happened next is how *not* strange it was for me. It wasn't distasteful, it wasn't even unpleasant or sad now. It was as if this were just a normal part of the cycle. I had cried for him when he was alive and, as I've said, there really was this deep sense of peace now. So it didn't seem odd or distasteful to me to pick him up and carry him to the Sherpa bag he normally used when he flew on planes with me. I will say that I did kiss him one last time, knowing that it would be the last time I was able to touch him, then I put him inside, zipped it up, got a towel and draped it over the bag.

When it was all done, I climbed back into bed and suddenly knew that I could, for the first time in days, maybe even weeks, go right to sleep. And not only that, I knew I could finally sleep soundly and deeply, and without the fear of what I'd wake up to find. The time for fear, as for pain, for both me and Norton, was past.

Janis came over first thing in the morning and we took Norton to the Washington Square Animal Hospital. The woman at the desk was expecting us and started to explain that Dr. DeLorenzo wasn't in quite yet but I explained that we'd come early and that we didn't need the doctor, that Norton had died already. I said that I just wanted to leave him there to be cremated.

She came around the desk and took the bag from me. I did have one last crying jag as I watched her carry him into the back. But it was only a brief one, nothing too drastic, and Janis held my hand and patted me lightly and comfortingly on the back, like one would do to a colicky baby, until I dried up. When the receptionist came back with the empty bag, Janis and I went outside into what was already becoming a hot and humid spring day. We went and had a huge breakfast at a diner on Bleecker Street. Tapping our orange juice glasses together, we had a bittersweet—and exhausted—toast to my sixteen and a half superb years of companionship.

I assumed that I'd now make a few calls, send a few e-mails, tell a few people, mourn for a little while, or even a long while, know that a small but valuable piece of me would be missing forever, but that things would go on much as before and that would be the end of it.

Uh-uh.

In death, my sweet, sweet cat continued to astound, possibly even more than he had in life.

The friends I called or e-mailed immediately called or e-mailed other friends, who contacted a whole other circle of people, and the next thing I knew I was getting calls from nearly anyone I'd ever met, talked to or heard about. Every close friend or relative who called sounded almost as sad as I felt. If there was any unanimity of sentiment in all these conversations, it was that all the people who called felt as if they themselves had lost a close friend.

A writer pal of mine, John Feinstein, another serious cat guy (he once flew home to Maryland from Paris, where he was covering the French Open tennis tournament, when one of his cats died suddenly), called and left this message on my phone machine: "I'm sure you're sad, but you shouldn't be *that* sad, because no cat ever had a better life." John's wife, Mary, sent me a wonderful note: "All the Feinsteins have been thinking of you. Yesterday Danny [their young son] asked if Norton could be his [Danny's] grandmother's cat in heaven. We figure anyone as widely traveled as Norton has found his way to the afterlife, and we told Danny a cat so well-loved would be unbeatable as a companion anywhere." Roman Polanski called from Paris to convey his condolences. "We had some great dinners together, Norton and I," he said wistfully. Norm Stiles, who probably knew Norton better than anyone outside of me and Janis, said, "It's amazing, isn't it, how our cats get into every minute aspect of our daily lives." And that's exactly the point that Janis made to me, when I began apologizing for how deeply sad I felt and how seriously I was grieving. "He wasn't just your cat," she had to explain to me. "You were with him practically twenty-fours a day. He was involved in your social life, your day-to-day life *and* your professional life. You didn't have that kind of all-consuming relationship with anyone else."

Young Charlie Alderman called and was his usual comforting self. "He died in a good way," he told me and I had to tell him that I agreed. His mom Nancy let me know a few days later that the Chuckster had been asked to write his autobiography for school. The ten-year-old's opening sentence was, "The first friend I ever had died when he was sixteen years old." He was, of course, referring to Norton, who was indeed one of his very first friends, meeting Charlie when the boy was days old.

Ben Eagle, the slightly-older-than-Charlie son of my best friend Paul, wrote and told me that he was dedicating a part of his own Web page to Norton.

Things started to get out of hand when a reporter

named James Barron from the *New York Times* called. He had heard about Norton's death (I believe from my agent, Esther, who had her own Scottish Fold, Tate, and was taking Norton's demise almost as hard as I was) and he wanted to write an obituary. I was taken aback but I must say, I liked the idea of Norton being the first cat to get an obit in the paper of record and I was positive that he would have loved it, too. Barron did a great job; he totally caught the spirit of my cat and our relationship. Best of all, he made it fun and funny, writing it as if Norton were a person, not a pet (which, of course, is the way I thought about him). I'll reprint it here, below, but I should point out my very favorite line, which comes at the end: "Besides Mr. Gethers, Norton is survived by Mr. Gethers's friend, Janis Donnaud." I think that's just perfect, and I know Norton would have liked that.

Naturally, even in death, Norton had to take center stage. Soon after the obit writer interviewed me, I got a call from a woman at the *Times* who said they would like a photo of Norton to run with the piece. I explained that I'd have to look to see what I had and she said that they were on deadline, they needed it quickly. I told her that if they could send a messenger, I'd have something ready, but she didn't know if they had time for that. She said she'd check and call me right back. Five minutes later, the phone rang again. It was the woman from the *Times*.

"Never mind," she said. "It turns out we have a photo of Norton on file here."

"Um . . ." I managed to say before she hung up again. "Just out of curiosity, do you have a photo of *me* on file there?"

"You don't want to know," was her answer.

NORTON

Recalling a Cat Who Got Around

Norton, a grayish cat with small, folded ears whose far-flung adventures were described in two books, died on Saturday. He was 16, said the person with whom he lived, the author **PETER GETHERS**.

He had kidney trouble and cancer, said Mr. Gethers, an executive at Random House who has also written novels and screenplays.

"He was a gift from an ex-girlfriend," Mr. Gethers said. "I didn't like cats at all. She brought him back from Los Angeles and gave him to me. It was an instant relationship."

Soon they were going everywhere together. One early trip was to a weeklong writers' conference in San Diego, Calif. During one workshop, **LEONA NEVLER**, an editor at Ballantine Books, became concerned that Mr. Gethers had left Norton (unattended and unleashed) by the swimming pool at their hotel.

"She couldn't get over why I wasn't worried," he said. "I went to the last place I had seen him and whistled, and he came out of the bushes."

Later Mr. Gethers told her that

Norton had flown on the Concorde, had lived in a hotel with views of the Parisian skyline (as well as open-window access to nearby rooftops) and had attended meetings with the director **ROMAN POLANSKI** and the actor **HARRISON FORD**.

She said, "You should write a book called 'The Cat Who Went to Paris,'" Mr. Gethers recalled yesterday. "I'm supposed to have my finger on the pulse of American culture, but I totally blew it off. I said, 'Right'"

But Ms. Nevler called Mr. Gethers's agent, **ESTHER NEWBERG**, and worked out a deal for the book. That first volume, published in 1991, was followed by "A Cat Abroad" (Crown, 1993).

Eventually, Mr. Gethers's traveling companion became so well known that mail addressed to "Norton, Sag Harbor, N.Y." was delivered — naturally, Norton had a place in the Hamptons. He was recognized throughout Europe. Once, on a walk through Amsterdam — Mr. Gethers was doing the walking; Norton was riding on his shoulders — someone stopped the pair and said, "Excuse me, is that the cat who went to Paris?"

It was. And as Mr. Gethers's readers came to understand, Norton was a cat with a distinct — and distinctive — personality. "He was independent without being standoffish," said Ms. Newberg.

Besides Mr. Gethers, Norton is survived by Mr. Gethers's friend, **JANIS DONNAUD**.

Once the *Times* announced my cat's departure from all things worldly, things got truly wild.

Various other news services picked up on the story, so Norton's death was written about in *USA Today* and, thanks to the Associated Press, printed in hundreds of local papers around the country. *People* magazine not only ran a full-page "Tribute" to my cat in the issue that came out ten days or so after his death, six months later they also included Norton in their special, year-end double-issue in the section "Notable Deaths." In this second story, Norton—depicted in a photo I took of him at Sweetwater Farm during our final trip together—was placed alongside the likes of Mel Tormé, Joe DiMaggio, Raisa Gorbachev, George C. Scott, Wilt Chamberlain, King Hussein, Stanley Kubrick and, I was particularly pleased to see, Señor Wences. My favorite part—this really made me chuckle as I knew it would have pleased my pal greatly—is that they didn't bother to identify him. They didn't say, "star of *The Cat Who Went to Paris*" or anything like that. They simply listed him, under his photo, as "A Literary Adventurer," gave his age as sixteen, and then got Rita Mae Brown to give a wonderful epitaph: "He was born a cat, but died a gentleman. His manners were perfect, and he was a very good traveling companion."

I couldn't have said it better myself.

I got a call from a friend, Linda, whom I hadn't spoken to in several months. She said that she'd heard about Norton's death and wanted to convey how very sorry she was. I asked if she knew about it because she'd read the

Times obit and she said no, she heard it on the radio. My exact response to this was, "*What?!!!*" and she then told me that she'd been driving into the city from her country house, was cruising along the Long Island Expressway listening to WCBS when, on the news, they announced that Norton—describing him as "the legendary Cat Who Went to Paris"—had died. She said she almost drove off the side of the road, but managed to compose herself as the station then went on and did a thirty-second tribute to the world's favorite Scottish Fold.

I called Janis immediately to tell her about this and then I had to shake my head. "You do realize," I told her, "that when *I* die no one's going to do a thirty-second tribute on the radio for *me*."

"Yes," Janis said, as sympathetically as she could muster, "I definitely realize that."

Letters and e-mails started pouring in. I am not exaggerating when I say that I received at least a thousand notes, each expressing sorrow and sympathy at Norton's passing. Writers I worked with, coworkers from the publishing business, more notes from friends. One writer who I published and also played with in the occasional game of poker, Bob Reiss, wrote: "I didn't think of him as your pet. I thought of him as your friend. Condolences in a time of grief." An agent, who I didn't know all that well but who had met Norton at various Random House meetings as well as at a couple of writers conferences, wrote: "He was the embodiment of otherworldly sophistication and his like won't be seen again. I mourn with you." Ann King, who took care of Norton the weekend Janis and I were in San Francisco, sent a note thanking me for letting her have the opportunity to spend those few days with him. I got letters from salespeople into whose stores I had taken Norton while I was shopping. The woman who bought my old apartment, and who had scratched and petted Norton while she was deciding whether she wanted to meet my asking price, sent these words: "Although I only met him twice, Norton left a lasting impression on me. He had an otherworldly quality about him, and I found myself telling everyone I knew about him. He really was a unique cat."

One of my favorite comments came from a dear friend, Becky Okrent, who sent a black and white postcard that was a photo of a cat standing on a young man's shoulder. The printed paragraph on the back of the card explained that the cat was Mrs. Chippy, a male cat who belonged to Henry Mcnish, an adventurer on the ship the *Endurance* during Shackleton's legendary arctic expedition. The man in the photo was not Mcnish but another sailor with Shackleton, Perce Blackbourne. Becky's note read: "Don't ask what happened to Mrs. Chippy when the crew was forced to abandon ship. But I hope he and Norton are sharing a few brews and tales of adventure in cat heaven."

Sharon MacIntosh, a friend and major cat lover, had these wise words to impart in an e-mail: "I think we're only allowed temporary guardianship of cats. Though I don't believe in heaven for people, I've always thought that all our good cats would meet up in cat heaven, where they'd have Fancy Feast, no fleas and MEOW MIX as often as they want. Most of all, I think cats—even more than humans—want to die with love and dignity. You gave Norton both."

When Norton's cancer had reached a fairly advanced stage, two of the few people I'd revealed this to were the women in Sicily, Wanda and Giovanna Tornabene, whose cookbook I'd published. Wanda, the mother, sent me the following fax when she first heard Norton was sick:

Dearest Peter,

Giovanna translated for me your letter and now she doing the same for my letter to you. You know how much I can understand your feeling about Norton. I have the same for my Puffo [her dog]. He is now 14 years and I can't imagine my life without him. So please give me, as often you can, news about Norton's health. Norton is not to me only your beloved cat. He is the mysterious go-between who gods decided to use to change, in some way, my life.

When Norton died, I got what I think are the most moving letters I've ever received, one from Wanda and one from her daughter. I am not changing a word of their English because while it is not technically perfect, it is, in fact, emotionally perfect. Wanda's note read:

Dearest Peter,

For my long experience, nothing can console you for the less of Norton, and nothing, for long time, will fill the empty he left in your heart and in your house. The truth, my dear friend, is that our little beloved animals are the mirror that reflects what we humans might be and often we are not. When they leave us, they bring with them our best part: the tenderness and all that enormous love, sometimes expressed just with a glance, secret words whispered in those little hairy ears, sure to be understood, the happy moments, the pains lived together. Norton had a wonderful life and he made your life wonderful. I am sure he teached you, about yourself, more than a thousand humans. I want to tell a story many years ago, after the death of my little cat, Lilli. I asked to my doctor and friend Vincenzo, "Do you think I am normal if, when I see to die an animal, I suffer more than when a human dies?" And I remember that he answered to me, smiling, "Not, you are not," then he added, "Maybe . . . maybe . . ." and his eyes became sad, surely he remembered his dog, Argo, buried on the top of a mountain in the Madonies, where today, with his ashes, Vincenzo sleeps, too. And often this, my "abnormality" brings me to suffer today, Peter, and your great pain is mine.

Love, Wanda.

Giovanna's note was on the same piece of paper, added to the bottom:

I've just translated my mamma's letter and, believe me, it has been so hard to write, crying, about Norton's death. To me he will be, forever, the ironic, independent creature who walked and danced over our restaurant tables years ago. To me he will be always alive in the Sicilian sun, as alive as will be our friendship.

Dr. Jonathan Turetsky sent me a wonderful note, part of which read, "I truly was saddened to hear of Norton's passing, although I know he was never particularly fond of me. I have learned, over the years, not to take too personally the resentment of some of my patients. I well realize that many don't easily grasp the concept of distasteful things being done 'for your own good,' and I content myself with the knowledge that, nevertheless, I am helping." He also enclosed a moving article which he'd written about the death of his dog several years ago. Marty Goldstein called and talked about Norton's spirit, which he said would never really leave me. And Dianne DeLorenzo's note said that, "In the short time I knew him he touched me deeply . . . Everyone should be so lucky to have a love like Norton in their lives. You both were blessed to have each other." Drs. Turetsky and Pepper and Dr. DeLorenzo and her partner Dr. Lucas sent donations in Norton's name (Turetsky's and Pepper's went to Tuft's University School of Veterinary Medicine; DeLorenzo's and Lucas's went to the University of Pennsylvania School of Veterinary Medicine). Actually, quite a few people made donations to animal hospitals and veterinary schools in Norton's name. I started to feel as if pretty soon I'd be running my own Labor Day telethon.

I got calls and letters from heads of companies and waiters who served Norton in restaurants and normally cynical, hard-bitten media people, all of whom had come into contact with my cat over the years. But, most astonishing, I got tons and tons of mail from total strangers who simply had to share their sadness and the fact that Norton had touched and even changed their lives.

Many of these letters were from people who felt the need to reach out and share my grief or tell me about their own losses. Most were sweet and compassionate and I truly was amazed at the degree to which Norton had entered their lives. I was equally amazed that so many people understood about Norton the way I thought only I understood. People wrote such things to me as "Needless to say, today's obituary in *USA Today* was a great shock to me and I've wept constantly all day," and "Knowing that Norton passed away I find myself with a gnawing sadness," and "Although I never did meet him in person, I felt I knew and loved him through his books" and "GOD!!! I'm still trying to recover from reading about Norton's death, which a friend sent to me over e-mail."

A huge number of the people writing told me about their own cats and the pain they experienced when those cats died. Many of those letters began with, "I had a Norton in my life" and then proceeded to tell me about the joys brought to them by their Mincemeat or Ju-Jube or their Snowball. Many of them also went on to detail tales of woe that included horrid diseases and sudden car accidents and runaway felines. Some of it was pretty morbid—but the intent, I know, was to show that whatever sadness I was feeling, I was not the only one who had experienced this. There was a cat community out there of which I was part—and at the center of which stood Norton.

A lot of people felt the need to simply pay tribute to their favorite feline and tell me they were sorry he was gone. Quite a number of them wrote to assure me that Norton was an "immortal cat" and would live forever not just inside me but in the minds and hearts of his fans. I soon discovered that various cat organizations, notably the Scottish Fold Association—needless to say Norton was a god amongst kittens as far as they were concerned—had posted the news of his death on their websites. Some even sent out special e-mailings to all of their members. These people were all shaken to the core. I got terrifically nice of-fers from breeders for a free cat if I ever decided to get an-other one. I got letters thanking me for showing them the way to happiness by introducing them to the Scottish Fold breed (I got so many of the latter that I was beginning to suspect I should do a book called *The Tao of Fold*). And I got plenty of letters similar to the one that just said, "I'm shocked. I don't know what to say. I hope you're doing well."

There was one couple who had written to me on a regular basis over the years. The first time I heard from them, they had told me that their young daughter had some mental and emotional problems. The only thing that con-sistently got her attention and made her smile was when they would read *The Cat Who Went to Paris* to her. As time passed, they would fill me in on their daughter's progress, which was considerable. The one constant was that she re-mained very attached to Norton. When he died, they told me how sad the girl was—but they also told me that she had made even more improvement. They absolutely gave credit to Norton for helping her make that improvement.

Several letters arrived—*quite* a few, actually—purport-edly written by cats. These typically began, "Dear Mr. Gethers, My name is Gingerbelle and I'm a 4-year Manx owned by Delilah Heffenpheffer. I was very sad to read about Norton's death as he was my idol."

I got one page of cat haikus, which I do have to say, made me laugh. I particularly liked:

Small, brave carnivores
Kill pine cones and mosquitos
Fear vacuum cleaner

and

> The rule for today:
> Touch my tail, I shred your hand.
> New rule tomorrow.

and

> Want to go outside.
> Oh no! Help! I got outside!
> Let me back inside!

But my favorite, no question, was this one:

> The Big Ones snore now.
> Every room is dark and cold.
> Time for Cup Hockey!

I got all sorts of cat cartoons and cat jokes, too, most of which were funny, although all the jokes almost always ended in, "And the dog was happy and the cat didn't give a shit."

Of course, there were a lot of spiritually oriented notes. Most of them were generous and warm and I was grateful for the good wishes they passed along

A lot of them said that they knew or suspected I did not share their beliefs but nonetheless they wanted to send me what they considered an appropriate prayer or poem or comforting thought. (Just for the record, I did get a few that brought up the whole "hell" subject again. The one I remember best was kind of taunting. It said that wasn't I sorry now, because Norton was definitely going to heaven but because I was such a heathen, I was definitely not. Too bad, he said, because if I'd been better I might have seen him again. But now . . . no chance! I thought about writing back to this fellow and asking him if he thought such extraordinary meanness was going to get him a place in good standing Up There, but I did the wise thing instead. I threw the letter away.)

Several people sent me information on pet loss support groups and pet loss counselors, which I also appreciated, but did nothing about. I couldn't imagine standing up in front of a bunch of other crying animal lovers saying, "Hi, I'm Peter. I'm catless."

One person sent me a copy of a page from the *Mayo Clinic Health Letter* which was devoted to pet loss and grief. This page had helpful little hints about what to say to a friend who's lost a pet. I learned that to console someone you do say, "I'm sorry to hear of your loss." You don't say, "You can always get another pet." Good tip, I thought.

That Mayo Clinic flyer also told me that I'd be surprised at the depth of my sorrow (they were right on the nose with that one, I'll give them credit for that), and that there were pet loss support hot lines, pet loss websites and books and videos which could all help me cope.

I had no idea that pet loss was such a big business. I was surprised to receive so many spiritual writings that were bought in stores and sold for just such an occasion. Most of them were not just about death and dying, they were specifically geared to the death of a pet. I got a ton of fancy cards that were engraved in very swirly writing with things like "We're sorry for the loss of your very special cat." Many of them seem to be made by a company called Pet Love (in their logo, the *o* in "love" is heart shaped). They featured a lot of photos of cats sitting in front of windows, with sunlight casting a heavenly glow about them. There were also quite a few peaceful cats lolling on fluffy pillows. The poems that were part of the cards were almost all about how we have to refill the food dish of life and pet the meowing spirit that lives on and let animal footprints dance gently on our heart forever.

I got many, many copies of an inspirational poem or essay—I'm not quite sure what it is—called "Rainbow Bridge." I mean, I probably got fifty of these in the mail. The sentiments are quite nice but whenever I got to the part about the meadows and hills where our special friends are playing, I'd get a little woozy. I always get woozy when I read the phrase "our special friends." Even though I did not believe that Norton had crossed over into heaven on Rainbow Bridge, I was glad to have seen this poem. It made me really confront my own feelings and define my own perspective. It got me to accept the fact that I really did believe that we live and we die and that even though the things in-between aren't always perfect they're what we've got and should be appreciated. End of story. While some people might not agree, that realization did indeed comfort me. I did not have to dream wistfully about joyful reunions in green, grassy fields somewhere up in the sky.

I grieved for my cat and grieve for him still. My comfort comes from the fact that I know and accept that my sadness is real. And heartfelt. I grieve for what I lost at the same time I celebrate what I had. I don't want to make myself feel better by pretending that there's more than there was to my relationship with Norton. Or that more is coming.

I don't need any more.

What we had was strong enough to last forever.

About a week after my cat died, I had to go pick up his ashes from the animal clinic. I can't say I was looking forward to this but when they called and said it was time, I walked over there and got him. The receptionist handed over a small, gray cardboard box that weighed practically nothing and was wrapped with a red ribbon, as if it were a Christmas present. On the label, I saw that this package came courtesy of the Pet Crematory Agency, Inc. And that it contained the "cherished pet of Peter Gethers: beloved Norton." Yes, for a change I did do a little sniffling, then left to take the remains of my cat home.

On the way back, I made a grand and sentimental gesture. I stopped off at the dog run in Washington Square Park. I settled on the bench that Norton and I usually sat on, held the box on my lap and leaned my head back, letting the bright sun hit my face. I stayed there for a decent amount of time then . . . well . . . to be honest, I felt a little silly. I'm not usually one for such gestures and I don't know why I went there. I suppose that partly it was another farewell. For me, sure, but also for Norton.

People had been asking me since his death if I was going to have a memorial service. At first I said no. I've made it more than clear how I feel about forced rituals, but I do have to say that the demand was overwhelming. Janis finally came to me and said that she thought it was a good idea. We had his ashes, she said, we were going to bury them, so let's do what he would have liked and have a little party. I still wasn't sure and told her I had to think about it.

A few days later, we were out in Sag Harbor for the weekend. I took out the cardboard box from the crematorium and opened it. Inside was a small, multicolored tin container. And inside that was what had once been my cat. Janis came up to me, put her hand on my back, and I told her that she should start calling people to invite them to a memorial on Sunday. When she asked what had changed my mind, I told her there were two things. One: I wanted to invite only those people who had actually shared a meal with Norton. I wanted to invite *his* friends. He had a lot of them and they all deserved the chance I'd had to say goodbye. The second thing I told her was that it was a chance to once and for all disprove Ziggy's favorite now-classic quote by my ex-girlfriend: "There are certain times that are inappropriate for humor." What I wanted to do, I said, was share with everyone who came, all the things that had happened since Norton died. I wanted them to feel as good as I did about the impact he'd had on people's lives. I wanted them to laugh the way I had, at so many things that had happened since that awful Saturday morning when he took his last breath.

So on Sunday morning, twenty-five people came over to our backyard. We ate a nice brunch outside, drank a little champagne, and then I delivered a short eulogy.

I've already mentioned how eulogy-readings are not my best thing. I did manage to get through this reasonably well. There were a few stops and starts and a lot of coughing in an attempt to hide my tremors. But except for the very, very end, when Janis had to step in and take over, I did it. I admitted that I felt a little foolish having a funeral service for a cat, said that I didn't know if I'd do it for a person, but I explained why I was doing it. And why they had been the ones invited. I talked about all the stuff that had occurred since May 8—the obits and the letters and weird poems and the amazing outpouring of affection. I got a few laughs and I don't think I was the only person in the yard shedding tears. And then I said I didn't think I could say anymore because I wouldn't just shed tears, I'd turn into that new comic book superhero, The Blubberer. I said that my cat loved this garden, so let's put him in it.

Which is what we did, burying him, scattering his ashes, under his favorite magnolia tree in the middle of his favorite garden.

As I write these final words, over a year and a half has passed since Norton died.

Letters and e-mails and calls are still coming on a regular basis. Some from people who just heard the news and are sending their shocked condolences. Some from people—people I've never met—who get in touch to tell me they're still thinking about me and about Norton and wondering how I am and if I've gotten another cat yet.

My favorite postfuneral letter came from a guy in Northern California who'd written a few fan letters after reading the first two books. When I opened the envelope, a twenty-dollar bill fluttered out. I fished out the letter and it said that this was the three-month anniversary of Norton's death and that I should use this twenty bucks to go out and get drunk.

I sent him back a thank-you note and with it I returned his money. But I did take his advice and had more than a few drinks to commemorate the sad occasion.

I have not gotten another cat yet. I'm not totally sure why. I think it's partly because I'm afraid. Norton was such an amazing animal and we had such an extraordinary bond, I don't know how I'd feel having a cat who wasn't quite so amazing or with whom I didn't have such a strong bond. I'm a little concerned that it would be like the lobster scene in *Annie Hall*. Things would be the same, but a little off. I'd take my new cat on a trip with me, expecting him to travel like Norton, and he'd freak out on the plane and be one of those cats you read about who spends three weeks living in the luggage compartment before being found by a janitor. The other thing that must be said is that it's somewhat freeing not having a cat. No responsibility. No lugging around portable litter boxes. No rushing home at night so he doesn't worry that I've been eaten by a predator. I'm sure I'll get one one day. When the time's right.

When I'm ready.

What happened to my cat—a long and happy life followed by a quick and fairly painless death—is not a tragedy. It is something that happens to everybody, in one way or another, sooner or later. Death defines life, and it's natural, and there's nothing we can do about it, but I suppose that I'm still grieving. The thing that eventually strikes you about the death of someone you love is the permanence. When that hits, there is an overpowering sense of loneliness and aloneness. Those wounds do not remain raw, not forever, but they do remain.

This past winter, I went back to Gangivecchio, spent a

month with my friends in Sicily writing a new book. It was wonderful but it was strange and sad to be there without Norton. I was fed like a king, met some eccentric Sicilians and heard some major stories. It was a productive, serene and, yes, I'll say it, almost spiritual experience. But every time I opened the door to my cottage, I half-expected my cat to be waiting there, meowing angrily that I'd forgotten to let him in. That kind of thing happens often. Soon after he died, hardly an hour went by that I didn't hear a noise and turn, expecting to find him rubbing up against the bed-post or trying to open the cupboard to get to a cat treat. When I'd sit at my computer to write, I'd automatically clear a space for him. Then I'd realize that he wasn't there to fill that space. I still do that occasionally. Not every time. Too many months have passed. But occasionally.

For a long time after Norton died, his little black friend kept coming over to the yard, looking for her pal. When he didn't come out to play, she would hang out by our back door, sometimes sneaking into the house to see if he was hiding. She still meanders into our yard, but I don't think she's looking for anything anymore. She just comes because it's a nice place for a cat to hang out and, if Janis and I are around, we pet her and tell her that she's looking mighty fine.

About a year ago, I went to stay at The Four Seasons Hotel in Los Angeles, one of Norton's all-time favorite haunts. It was a nightmare. I pulled up in my car and the parking guy gave a big smile and said, "Welcome back, Mr. Gethers. Is Norton with you?" I quietly mumbled no, that I was sorry to say that he'd died. When I got to the door, the doorman said the same thing, "What, no cat?" Again, I shook my head, felt a little self-conscious, and said, "No, no, my cat died." As I walked through the lobby, the concierge called out to me, "Where's Norton?" and so did one of the bellmen who had carried many bags of cat litter up to the room for me. By the time I got to the desk clerk, who did nothing more than smile and say hello, I couldn't stand it, and I screamed out, "He's dead! Okay! He's *dead*!!!!"

I'm not nearly as welcome now at The Four Seasons as I was when Norton stayed there with me.

Several months ago, I had occasion to call Sweetwater Farm. I told Rick, the owner, that Norton had died and he said, just like this, "We had a death around here, too." I expected him to tell me that the goat had passed on, but when I asked who it was he said, "Grace." I said, "Grace, your *wife*?" And he said, yes, that a few months earlier she'd had a stomachache. It went on for three days, got really bad, so she went to see a doctor. She had stomach cancer. And three weeks later she was dead.

The woman who called to tell me she'd heard Norton's obit on WCBS radio, she died recently, too. It doesn't just happen to cats, you know. An old friend of mine died of AIDS. A close friend's brother died in a plane crash.

Things change. People die. But life goes on.

It's different. But it goes on.

And it can be just fine.

The Spring Trip this year was to Cuba, as thrilling a place as I've ever been. We smoked cigars and consumed a lot of aged rum, met kind and brave people, and heard magnificent, sensual salsa music. We didn't just toast Belle at our Saturday night dinner. This year we drank a *mojita* to a small, gray Scottish Fold and we all felt particularly lucky to be where we were and with close friends and to just be having a damn good time.

A few weeks ago, Janis and I went to Paris. Had dinner with Roman Polanski and his wife Emmanuelle, saw their two gorgeous children, stayed at the Tremoille Hotel. We ate the amazing chicken and even more amazing potato pie at L'ami Louis, and it doesn't get any better than that. We shopped, we strolled around all our favorite neighborhoods, we pretended we spoke French. It felt like old times. Except that woman with the antique shop, the one where I saw Marcello Mastroianni? That store's gone now. And except for the fact that several times I came down the steps at the Tremoille and saw a cat sitting in a chair in the lobby and each time I thought: *It's Norton, how did he get out of the room?*

And then I remembered that he didn't get out of the room.

But mostly what I remember about my cat is how much better my life is because he was in it.

Norton, throughout his lifetime, made many things possible for me, and he taught me about many things. About love and about relationships. About adventure. About independence. At the end of his life, he showed me that it's possible to die with dignity and grace. And, to a certain extent, that it's possible to end one's life on one's own terms. Ultimately, what my cat showed me is that it's possible to die with love and without fear, and that's a pretty damn valuable lesson.

It means that even with the sadness that's sure to come, life can never really get too bad.

Several weeks after he died, I ordered a small stone marker for his grave in the garden. Engraved on it is:

NORTON
T.C.W.W.T.P.

So some of you don't have to puzzle over the letters for the next several weeks, they stand for "the cat who went to Paris."

The marker is still there, will remain there as long as I own the house. I don't go out to look at it every day that I'm in Sag Harbor but I do go from time to time. Usually, just for a few seconds. I'll stand or I'll sit on the small wooden bench that's on the grass nearby.

Most of the time, when I see the grave, I have tears in my eyes.

Always, when I see the grave, I smile.